To Jeff
Great to
see you
& God Bless!

Jim

Jobb —
Best wishes!
John Weber
March, 2007

Real American Heroes
Secrets To Their Success

by

John Weber
and Jim Gibbs

authorHOUSE™

1663 LIBERTY DRIVE, SUITE 200
BLOOMINGTON, INDIANA 47403
(800) 839-8640
WWW.AUTHORHOUSE.COM

© 2004 John A. Weber and James Ward Gibbs. All Rights Reserved.

No part of this book may be reproduced, stored in a retrieval system, or transmitted by any means without the written permission of the authors.

First published by AuthorHouse 01/28/05

ISBN: 1-4208-1040-5 (sc)

Printed in the United States of America
Bloomington, Indiana

This book is printed on acid-free paper.

Dedication

To Carol Weber and Karen Gibbs, our two heroes.

Also, to everyone who lives and works in both Lesterville, South Dakota and Glen Rose, Texas, the home towns of authors John Weber and Jim Gibbs, respectively.

Many people seem to forget that, in a small town, everyone is a hero to someone. The authors are thankful to all those they grew up with and how, in even the smallest way, their lives were touched by various people in those communities.

Acknowledgements & Authors' Notes

The authors would like to gratefully acknowledge the help of all of the great men and women who are mentioned in this book and want to take this opportunity to thank them for allowing us to interview them and tell their stories.

All of the *Real American Heroes* mentioned in this book are unique, yet all share a sense of humility, graciousness and an enthusiasm for life that was both refreshing and inspiring.

We would also like to thank all of the secretaries, agents and public relations staff members who helped us to set up interviews with these *Real American Heroes* so that we could include them in this book.

Dave Branon, the editor extraordinaire at *Sports Spectrum Magazine*, also played a key role in this book. Many of the stories that you see here originally appeared in *Sports Spectrum Magazine* during the early 1990s and Dave was gracious enough to allow us to reprint them here.

C.A. "Al" Gregory of Easton, Maryland helped us edit the book and Kelly Wise did a brilliant job with the design for the cover.

Maria Villa and Rebecca Bair of Glen Rose, Texas illustrated many of the Heroes that you see here and the authors gratefully acknowledge their help. The Late Mrs. Thomas Eakin painted the portrait of Brooks Robinson that appears with Robinson's story and also did the sketch of Jim Sundberg.

Our good friend Teresa Slupski took the photo for the back cover and we appreciate her work.

Last, but not least, we would like to thank our families, who were the true "heroes" when it came to publishing a book like this. Their support made this possible and we are both eternally grateful.

In His Grace,
John Weber and Jim Gibbs

Foreword

Heroes. We've all had one at one time or another.

When I was growing up in Galesburg, Illinois, my heroes were all baseball players. I wanted to be just like them.

Fortunately, I got to live my dream of playing professional baseball for the Texas Rangers and, later, for the 1985 World Champion Kansas City Royals.

And one of the things that I have learned during more than 30 years of playing, broadcasting and coaching professional baseball is how important role models are for people. That's why I'm proud to be a part of this book that John Weber and Jim Gibbs have put together.

Obviously, I enjoyed reading the stories about some of the great athletes of our time and what made them successful, but it was also interesting to read some thoughts from people like Dave Thomas, the founder of Wendy's, who talked about success and the perils often associated with it.

In this book, you'll read about Colin Powell's stickball playing days in the streets of New York, meet the lady behind former NFL running back Tommie Agee's success, hear from Reggie White, the NFL's Minister of Defense and also hear some pretty strong Christian testimonies from myself and basketball superstar David Robinson.

You'll also be introduced to the rigors of the music industry by two musical icons of the 1950s, 60s and 70s – Pat Boone and Gladys Knight -- and hear from many, many other heroes that you only thought you knew.

I hope you have as much fun reading this book as I did and, remember, everybody is a hero to somebody.

- JIM SUNDBERG

Table of Contents

Tommie Agee
  Agee's Secret Weapon 5

Mary Kay Ash
  Flight of the Bumblebee! 13

Pat Boone
  Hip To Be Square 21

Dr. Ben Carson
  The End of a Terrible Temper 31

Steve Cauthen
  The Kid From Walton 37

Tony Dungy
  Heart of a Champion 51

Thomas Fleming
  Super Teacher 67

Chad Hennings
  A Lesson In Commitment 81

Gladys Knight
  Just Gladys 89

Tom Landry
  Amazing Grace 97

Bob Lilly
  The Dangers of Alcohol 107

Jim Lovell
> *Bilirubin Blues* *117*

Russell Maryland
> *Man At Work* *123*

Johnny Oates
> *Deep in the Heart of Texas* *129*

Colin Powell
> *Back in the Bronx* *137*

Bobby Richardson
> *Winter Meeting* *147*

Brooks Robinson
> *Oriole Magic* *159*

David Robinson
> *Mr. Robinson's Neighborhood* *165*

Jim Sundberg
> *Man Behind the Mask* *175*

Dave Thomas
> *"You're Fired!"* *179*

Reggie White
> *Minister of Defense* *189*

Gordon Wood
> *Winning Values, Winning Ways* *197*

Zig Ziglar
> *Tips From The Top* *209*

EARLY BEGINNINGS - Co-author Jim Gibbs and his hero, Brooks Robinson, in April of 1977. (See *Oriole Magic*, Page 159)

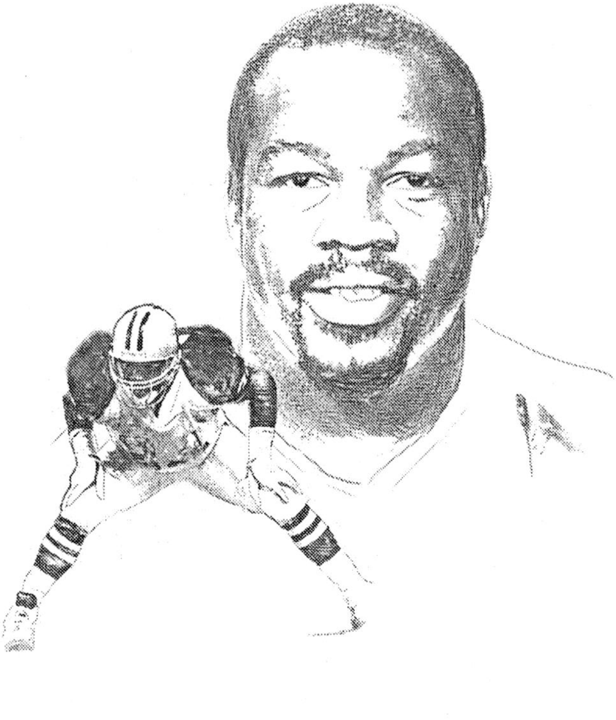

Tommie Agee

Agee's Secret Weapon

The chances are good that you'll never see former Dallas Cowboys running back Tommie Agee enshrined into the National Football Hall of Fame in Canton, Ohio. But when you consider Agee's humble beginnings, it's amazing he ever made it to the National Football League at all. Shortly after the Cowboys had won their second Super Bowl of the 1990s, Agee spoke candidly about the woman behind his dream of playing in the NFL.

From growing up in the small town of Maplesville, Alabama to playing on two Super Bowl Championship teams, Tommie Agee had come a long way.

But he didn't do it alone.

True, even as a youngster, he was far above his peers both academically and athletically. But, then again, unfulfilled potential litters the landscape of high school, college and professional sports.

So what or who made the difference? He played alongside some of the greatest players in the game, including

Heisman Trophy winner Bo Jackson at Auburn University and Troy Aikman, Emmitt Smith and Michael Irvin with the Dallas Cowboys. He even played for celebrated Coach Jimmy Johnson.

But if you asked Agee who the most important person in his life was, he'd say it was a faithful and consistent grandmother.

At 64 years old, Helen Morris had never been to an NFL game. Yet, she still played a major role in her grandson's life.

"Grandma always monitored my comings and goings," Tommie said, smiling that big smile of his. "She was there walking softly but carrying a big stick."

Unlike many children from modern homes, Tommie says he refuses to play what he calls the "blame game."

Early in his career, Agee could often be found at the local Department of Youth Services in Montgomery, Alabama, where he warned teenagers about the dangers of drugs and the benefits of staying in school.

"When I was a young boy, I learned pretty quickly that I was responsible for what I did," Agee recalls. "In talking to young people, I find that too many of them want to blame their environment or their parents for the problems that they are having now. They've made some bad choices and kids have to realize that, when they do make a bad decision, they have no one to blame but themselves."

Those bad decisions, like deciding to try drugs or alcohol for the first time, often lead kids down a path that is tough to walk away from, Agee said.

"Seventy-five to 80 percent of the kids I talked to at the correctional facility in Montgomery are guys who got into drugs because someone told them to try it one time," he said. "So they try it once, then they try a little more the next time and, before you know it, they're hooked. And drug habits get expensive. The next thing you know they're out stealing money from people to try to support their drug habit. What they don't realize is, had they just made the right choice initially when someone first offered them drugs, they could have avoided all the problems that they are going through now."

Maplesville High School in Maplesville, Alabama only had about 200 students when Agee graduated from there in 1982. In fact, Agee's graduating class only had 35 students in it. Yet, as small as it was, there was also a lot of accountability there that Agee said helped him set his values at an early age.

"No matter what you did, everybody knew about it," he said. "If you did something good, people knew. And, if you did something bad, people also knew. We were afraid to get into too much trouble because if I got a spanking at home, everybody at school would know it the next day. That's just the way it is in a small town."

So when another boy would come up to Tommie and offer him an illegal drug of any sort, it seemed almost second nature for Agee to shrug off the temptation much like he would an oncoming tackler in a football game.

"I'd just come right out and tell them that I didn't want to do it," he said. "I would tell them that I've made it this far without drugs and I've made a commitment to myself to stay drug-free. I don't need drugs to be successful."

By today's standards, one probably wouldn't consider Maplesville, Alabama a mecca of entertainment. Yet, for a kid growing up in the late 1960s and 1970s, there were a million things to do on a Saturday afternoon or after a long day at school.

"There was this wooded area near our house that we called 'The Jungle,'" Agee said, smiling. "There were all kinds of vines and a little river there and we would swing across the river with those vines. Man, those vines would put the swings that they had at school to shame. It was great fun. Dangerous, but fun."

Games of kickball and basketball were also common in Agee's neighborhood, as the kids on the block would often collect enough money to buy a basketball goal and then put it up in a central location and play a game of "hoops."

"We would play baseball with broomsticks and rubber balls and just make up a lot of games to play," Agee said. "It seemed like we were always doing something like that - shooting baskets into an old goal, hitting rubber balls with broomsticks, playing kickball in a neighbor's garage. We were always into something. It was always good clean fun, but we were always into something."

It was during a friendly kickball game in first grade that Tommie almost lost a front tooth. As it was, he still lost part of one.

"We were playing kickball in our neighbor's carport and were using the poles for bases," he said. "I kicked the ball and somebody yelled something. I looked back to see who said it and ran right into the pole that was supposed to be first base. The pole chipped one of my front teeth and, from that point on, I was always a little bit self-conscious about it. You could see it when I smiled so, as a result, I didn't smile too much because I didn't want anybody to see my tooth."

It wasn't until he went to Auburn University that he finally got that tooth fixed.

"It was a great relief to finally get that taken care of," he said. "When I was a kid, my parents just didn't believe in going to the dentist so I went all through elementary, junior high and high school with that chipped tooth. It was very embarrassing to me. I felt like everybody was always looking at it. To a certain extent, I think it did make me a little bit shy growing up. I tried not to laugh or smile too much when I was younger because I didn't want it to show. Now, though, I'm smiling all the time. I think I'm trying to make up for all those times I couldn't smile as a kid."

At first glance, it would appear that Agee had very little to smile about when it came to his situation at home. His parents would often argue and, many times, his mother would leave the house, leaving Tommie's father, Arthur, to take care of Tommie and his three brothers. When this would happen, there would often be long periods of time when Tommie seldom saw either of his parents.

His grandmother, however, was always there for him.

"When Mom would leave the house after an argument with Dad, Dad would be in charge of the kids by himself," Agee said. "He couldn't take care of us kids by himself, so he would take us over to Grandma's."

It was at his grandmother's house that Agee learned the value of hard work. He also learned how important it was to put others before himself.

"My grandmother never saw me play football when I was in high school," Agee said. "She was too busy working and taking care of her elderly brothers. She could have put her brothers in a nursing home but, instead, she felt like they would be better off staying with her. I'll never forget how unselfish she was in caring for them."

His grandmother also taught Tommie the importance of going to church and building a daily relationship with Jesus Christ.

"My parents were Christians but when I was growing up they didn't make a strict habit of going to church every

Sunday like my grandmother did," Agee said. "When we would stay with her, we went every Sunday. Period. I don't care if there was a party on Saturday night, we were supposed to have our Sunday school lesson read in time for church and Sunday school the next day. And I just loved it. It was hard to get used to at first but once I got into the habit of going, I wouldn't have missed going to church with Grandma for anything in the world. I just ate it up."

Tommie's parents have solidified their relationship over the years and his mother has even become a minister.

"Mom and Dad have been back together now for more than 15 years," Agee said. "They've picked up the pieces and they've become very good parents."

Tommie Agee didn't have the perfect childhood. But, through Christ and an amazing gift for seeing the good in even the worst of circumstances, Agee was able to achieve what many others with similar gifts could not.

"Even though my parents didn't have the perfect relationship, I was still able to learn a lot from them," he said. "From my mother, I learned not to abandon my family when things got tough. From my older brothers I learned the value of staying in school since two of my older brothers didn't finish high school."

Both of those brothers could have played professional or at least college football, Agee said.

"Any of them could have gone on to play big-time college football," he said. "They were both better players than I was. But they wanted to get out on their own, become independent. So they left high school and never came back. It was only later that they realized that, without an education, there was no way that they could achieve the means to become independent. They made me stay in school. In fact, they all insisted on seeing my report cards. They would always say, 'Make it for us.'"

So Agee did. He graduated from high school with honors and also graduated from Auburn University.

Perhaps more than anything else, his career in the NFL has taught him just how important education is.

"The statistics are incredible," Agee said, "At my position (running back) the average career in the NFL is about three years. You can't play football forever and I'm glad I've prepared myself for a career after football with a college degree."

After the 1994 season, Agee retired from football with two Super Bowl rings and a lifetime of memories.

Like the old song goes, Tommie accentuated the positive, eliminated the negative and forgot about Mr. In-Between.

He also refused to play the "blame game."

"I learned I couldn't control Mom and Dad," he said. "But I could control myself and my own attitude. My parents have become a lot wiser over the years, largely because of the difference that Christ has made in each of their lives."

And Tommie's grandmother?

"She's got a job now!" Tommie says, in mock disbelief. "She helps other housekeepers cook. People keep telling her she should retire but she still insists on helping others. That's why I guess she'll always be my hero."

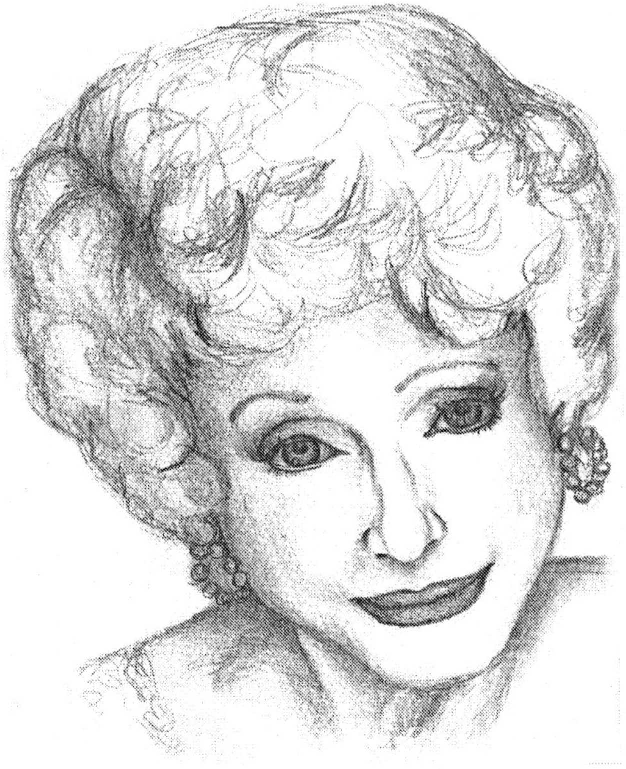

Mary Kay Ash

Flight of the Bumblebee!

Mary Kay Ash was just as friendly on the phone when we talked to her as she was when she was marketing her outstanding line of cosmetics. We caught up with her in the early 1990s and she was still going strong as she let us in on just a few of her secrets to running a successful organization. She died on November 22, 2001 but not before becoming an inspiration to women around the world.

At first glance, a visitor at the Mary Kay Cosmetics offices in Dallas might be taken aback by the unusual diamond bumblebee pins worn by many of the company's employees.

But when you think about how God designed the bumblebee, with its large body and small wings, it's a design that defies every law of aerodynamics.

Yet somehow it does fly and this is the story of Mary Kay Ash.

After almost four decades, it's hard to imagine a time when Mary Kay Cosmetics were not a part of the beauty culture.

Since 1963, Mary Kay Ash's fine line of beauty products and cosmetics have helped millions of women not only appear more beautiful but also become financially independent.

By the mid-1990s, Mary Kay Cosmetics was a billion (that's "b" as in bumblebee) dollar company with offices worldwide. Today, there is hardly a woman in the United States who hasn't heard of Mary Kay or hasn't tried Mary Kay's unique brand of cosmetics.

But it hasn't always been this way. In fact, it almost didn't happen.

"We didn't get off to the best of starts," recalls Ash. "My husband died on August 13, 1963, exactly one month before we were supposed to start the business. Suddenly, I had a decision to make. Do I go on with my plans for the business or do I forget about those plans and go to work for someone else?

"My son Richard said he would quit his job and come to Dallas and help me. I offered him the tremendous sum of $250 per month if he would help me. My other son told me that he thought I could do anything that I put my mind to and that he wanted to give me the $4,500 that he had saved so that we could go ahead with the business because we were literally out of money. Then, my daughter offered to go to work for me, too. So, with all of that, we decided to go ahead and start the company in September of 1963. Over the years, we've grown to the point where, now, we're a $1.7 billion company."

Mary Kay's business success, she quickly points out, is largely due to her mother.

"It all goes back to my mother," she said. "My mother was constantly telling me that I could do anything that I wanted to if I wanted it badly enough and was willing to pay the price. 'You can do it' was the philosophy of my childhood and it just carried on into my adulthood. I just think that it is terribly important for kids to realize that, no matter what it is in life that they want to do, they really can do it and they need someone to pat them on the back and tell them that."

Mary Kay added that, many times, young people are not aware of the sacrifices that parents make for them.

"When I was growing up, my mother really couldn't afford for me to take ballet and tap dancing lessons and some of those different things that I wanted to do but, somehow, she managed to pay for them anyway. Then, when I needed a typewriter, she managed to get me one. In those days, to us, that was like buying a car. Yet, she managed to do it and I began to realize how much she was giving up to make all of these things happen for me.

"I think that one of the problems that we have today is that kids are given so much that they don't really appreciate what their parents are giving up to make all these things possible. Not just financially, but also in time and energy. I was aware of the sacrifices that my mother made but I'm not sure that many of today's kids are aware of what their parents are giving up. They just want those $180 tennis shoes and, if they don't get them, they feel badly about it."

Mary Kay entered the business world almost by accident. She certainly wasn't looking for a job, yet destiny seemed to intervene as she soon found herself selling child-rearing books door-to-door.

"My first job came about in a rather unusual way," she explained. "At that time, I had three small children and a woman came by to sell me some books. They cost $50. That was absolutely out of reach as far as I was concerned. But I really liked the books and, when the woman realized that I couldn't afford to buy the books myself, she thought maybe I could sell some for her. She left the books for me over the weekend and I just fell in love with them. They were great books and I realized that they could help me so much with my own kids. They had things in them like what to do if a child told a fib and how to handle that situation without breaking the child's morale or whatever. They were great! The lady told me that if I sold 10 sets of books, she would give me a complete set. Well, to me, that was manna from heaven.

"At the time, I was superintendent of the Beginner Sunday School class and I knew a lot of people who could use those books. I got on the phone and started calling the beginner children's parents and, over the phone, began to sell the books. Well, when the woman came back to my house on Monday, I gave her a list of ten people who wanted the books. She didn't believe me at first because the books were expensive and they were hard to sell. But she soon found that the list was perfect and she sold the books to each of the 10 people on that list.

"She was so excited that she gave me the books and then told me that she wanted me to go to work for her. Well, good heavens! I thought. Go to work for her indeed! She asked me if I had a car and I told her that my husband had one but that I didn't know how to drive. So she told me to tell him to leave the car for me the next day and get someone to watch the kids because I was going to go out with her and sell some books.

"Well, up to that point, it had been pretty easy to sell the books, so I agreed. The next morning she showed up and we spent the entire morning canvassing a little subdivision. Ninety percent of the time, we couldn't even get past the front door. People were literally slamming the door in my face!

"Then, on the way home, she got out of the car and got in on my side and told me that I was going to drive home.

I told her that I didn't know how to drive and she said that I was going to learn. So we drove home in the five o'clock traffic in downtown Houston. Needless to say that it was a pretty bumpy ride home because that was the time before automatic transmissions and I had never driven a stick shift before. Somehow, though, we made it home."

The next day, Mary Kay ran up a curb and knocked down three pillars in front of the restaurant where her mother worked.

"That didn't discourage me, though," she said. "I was back out there driving the next day."

She was also back out there selling, but not door-to-door.

"I learned not to go door-to-door anymore," she said. "After that dreadful first day, I immediately began to think of new ways to sell the books. I went home and started calling more people from Sunday school who I thought might be interested. I sold to people that I knew. I didn't try to sell to strangers. I got people I knew to buy the books and then got them involved in it to the point where they were recommending the books to their friends."

It was from this small beginning that Mary Kay Ash began her career in sales and, later, would spend 25 years working her sales magic for the Stanley Home Products Company.

Stanley, like Mary Kay Cosmetics, is based on the "In-Home" demonstration.

"You host parties, people show up and, hopefully, people will buy your products," Mary Kay said.

Shortly after Mary Kay had retired from Stanley, she began to consider the idea of starting her own company. She needed a new product. Something unique. Something that people could use every day.

In the early 1950s, at a Stanley Home Products Party, she couldn't help but notice the "perfect" complexion of each of the ladies in attendance.

"After my sales presentation, we gathered in the kitchen for coffee, and it was there that I noticed my hostess handing out little white jars with black tops and penciled labels," Ash writes in her book, *Mary Kay*. "As she distributed the items, she made notations in a composition book and gave instructions such as 'Now, let's see, you've used number three for two weeks, so use number four for 17 days.'"

That night, Mary Kay took a shoebox full of the creams home with her and, over the next few weeks, was amazed with the results. By 1963, she had become a loyal fan of the products and had purchased the original formulas.

She was convinced that she had a great product. But there was still some uncertainty as to whether or not it was the right business for her.

"I knew how to sell and how to recruit, but I didn't know a lot about cosmetics at that time," she said. "But I chose cosmetics because it was something that women could sell if they believed in them and we needed a product that people had to come back for and it was on that basis that we started."

As her business began to grow, her free time decreased. She was not only the owner of Mary Kay Cosmetics, she was also a wife who had responsibilities to her new husband, Mel Ash.

"Somewhere, I read that getting up two hours earlier every day could add an extra day to my week, so I started getting up at 5 a.m. every day. And I began doing that, even when I didn't have a list of things to do. I could just get more done. I would get up and write letters or do whatever I needed to do.

I could do more between the hours of 5 a.m. and 7 a.m. than I could between 7 a.m. and noon."

Balance. Perspective. If Mary Kay has learned anything over the years, it is that these two ingredients are essential for success.

"Our philosophy has always been God first, family second and work third," she said. "I knew that I had to give my husband the attention that he needed while, at the same time, getting the things done at work that I had to get done. Somehow, when you start thinking in that direction, miracles happen. I always arranged ahead of time what we were going to have for dinner and our meals were either ready-to-cook or pre-cooked and frozen. That way, I would be able to heat it up and have it ready for Mel when he came home. We would have roast or casseroles or things like that.

"It was tricky because we didn't have a maid around to cook dinner. He thought that was something that we should be doing for ourselves. I'd have a casserole defrosting in the refrigerator so that it would be ready to stick into the oven when I got home and I would serve it and we would sit down and have dinner together. That was very important to our relationship."

God first, family second and work third. That may be as close as we get to the secret of the bumblebee's flight.

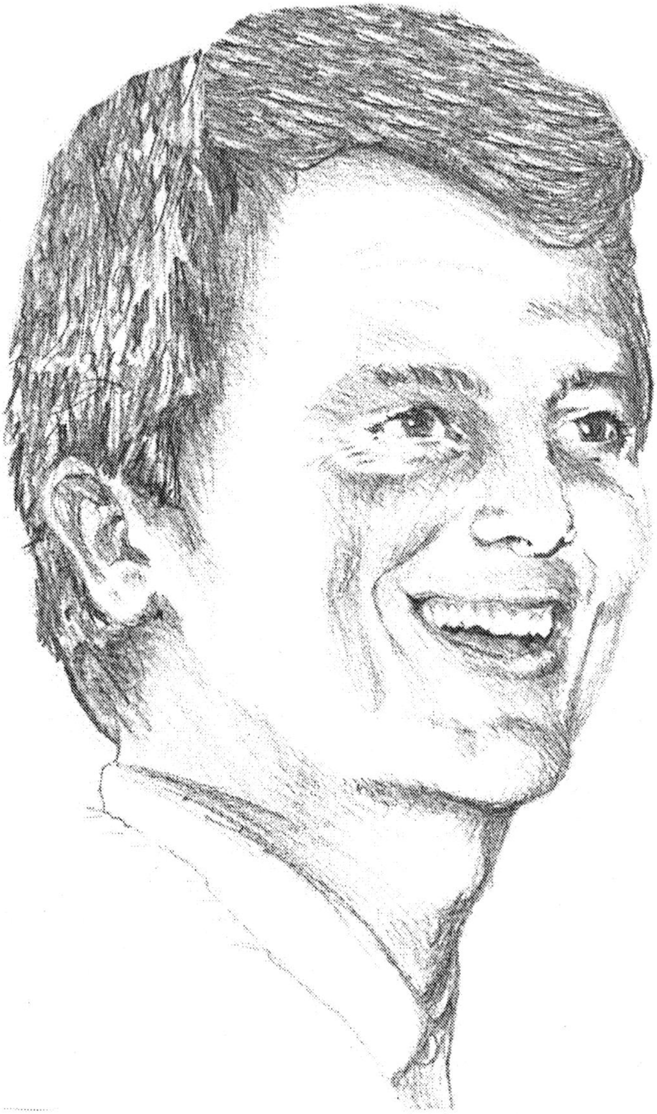

Pat Boone

Hip To Be Square

Growing up, Baby Boomers idolized Pat Boone. When youth of the turbulent 1960s would feel peer pressure to do things they shouldn't, they could pick up one of Pat's books such as Twix Twelve and Twenty *or* A New Song *and get back on track. In June of 1994, we talked to Pat while he was in Branson, Missouri, where he was playing the role of Will Rogers in a reprise of the Will Rogers Follies. Unlike many celebrities, he's not afraid to take a stand for Christ in an entertainment industry that has often crossed the boundaries of good taste. How did he do it and stay true to his principles? Read on my friend.*

Pat Boone showed that it was hip to be square in an entertainment world that was constantly changing.

Long before most of America knew who Pat Boone was, Boone had never been one to turn down any opportunity of any kind, no matter how big or how small.

"I accepted many opportunities to sing when it didn't look like they meant anything at all professionally," he said.

"They were freebies and they were favors to people and some of that, of course, was not having the discipline to say 'No' to things along the way. If I didn't have a legitimate reason for not doing it, and could work it in, I usually tried to find a way to help them out and do it for them. You would think that would be robbing me in some ways and deflecting me from my goals but it has worked the other way. As I gave of my time and my talents, they multiplied and came back to me. There's a spiritual principle at work there and I think it was true in my case."

But while Boone was always available for guest appearances on such programs as "The Arthur Godfrey Show" and other popular programs of the 1950s and 1960s, he was also quick to draw the line on hosting programs that were sponsored by beer or cigarette companies. It was just not the image that he wanted to project.

While other entertainers would have jumped at the chance to host their own TV show, no matter who sponsored it, Boone stood "pat." If the only sponsors they could find for a television show were beer and cigarette companies, then the networks would have to find another host.

To the contemporary music industry, that was "square" thinking in the "hip" world of entertainment.

"In the beginning, singing was a hobby and a dream," he said. "I went about what I thought would be the best use of my life as I pursued a career in education and in the ministry. I was already married and pretty soon we were expecting our first child.

"But God knew my heart and he led me to these jobs as a performer as a means of working my way through school so that by the time I was actually out of school, these 'get-through-school jobs' had become my vocation.

"So when young people ask me how to get ahead in show business, I first tell them to make God their agent. Most agents ask for 10 or 15 percent and God only asks for 10. But you should always make Him your agent because He can open doors that no other agent can and He can create opportunities that no other agent can. He gave you the talent to begin with and it may be that He has a better idea of how that talent can be used than you do. So trust Him to lead you in that direction."

Boone should know. He followed his own advice, although it made him a "square" in the "hip" entertainment world.

"That's what happened to me," he said. "I made up my mind what I thought I could do and what I thought would be worthwhile and I headed in that direction. But I was praying about it all the time and God knew my heart. He knew that He could use me as an entertainer and that's what I really wanted to be. So, without my having to strain or fret, when I look back over my career, I realize that the major, most important events in my life were simply saying 'yes' to opportunities that were presented to me."

One of those opportunities early in Boone's career arose when a new sponsor - Chevrolet - came along and made him the host of the "Chevrolet Amateur Talent Hour." Other shows began to call and it wasn't long before Pat Boone and his white buckskins were a household symbol for the All-American Boy of the 1950s.

By the end of the 1960s, however, there was a new mood in America. President Kennedy and Martin Luther King had been assassinated. There were race riots in several parts of the country and the protests over the war in Vietnam divided the United States in a way not seen since the Civil War.

It was at about that time that movie producer Ray Stark came along and offered to buy Boone's movie contract from Twentieth Century Fox. Stark wanted to change Boone's "square" image and Pat was agreeable.

"I had read that Dick Powell (star of the old *Thin Man* series) had started his career as a singer, had enjoyed terrific popularity, and then had changed his image in mid-career with a dramatic role as a private detective," Boone wrote in his book *Together* (Thomas Nelson, 1979). "Why couldn't I do the same thing? What did Paul Newman and Steve McQueen have that I didn't have -- except a totally different kind of image and some acting talent."

Stark's first big project for Boone was a film called *The Main Attraction* in which Boone would play an immoral drifter who wandered into a circus and fell in love with an oriental beauty. The script seemed harmless and Boone accepted the assignment.

That is, it seemed harmless until he returned home from Europe and found that the script had been rewritten to fit into a society that had forgotten its code of ethics.

Boone threatened to walk off the set unless the script was rewritten. Unfortunately, he was under contract. If he walked out, he could be sued.

Reluctantly, Boone made the film, which went on to be one of his few box-office flops.

"That was a time when I quit letting God be my agent," Boone said. "That was a time when I thought I could take things into my own hands and that God really didn't know anything about show business. I had forgotten that the Lord had put me in show business to begin with and, against all odds, had opened doors that I had never known to exist, much less how to get through. I just began to think that I knew about show business and things like that.

"I began to think, 'I'm not going to have a very long career as a singer if they're not making singing movies. Besides, I think my image is a little bland and one-dimensional and I need to expand it.' So, I started trying to do that. I took a role and accepted a contract in a movie. Of course, I didn't create the contract, I just accepted it. So, once I went along with the idea that perhaps I would do better by changing my image instead of just being what I had always been, whether it was necessarily popular or not, I got into trouble because I started to not only change my image professionally but I also tried to change my image privately, or personally, and fell into some of the same traps that a lot of entertainers do. That is, moral and spiritual traps and buying into counterfeit things and acting like I was a really 'hip,' sharp and aware person."

Boone was being "hip" – but it was not working for him.

If it was a difficult time for Boone, it was perhaps an even more difficult time for his producers. In *The Main Attraction*, Boone was supposed to have the rugged look of a motorcycle badboy with a five-o'clock shadow. Not exactly a beard, but not exactly the smooth-faced Boone that moviegoers were accustomed to seeing. Boone's beard, however, would not cooperate. After a few days worth of growth, he could manage only a few stray whiskers. The make-up artist, in an act of desperation, finally rubbed cigarette ashes and ground up cork into Boone's thin beard, hoping for the desired effect.

Suffice it to say that the new image was not working. It was not working at the studio and, more importantly, it wasn't working at home with his wife Shirley and their four daughters.

After a great deal of introspection and a lot of prayer, Boone came to the same conclusion that Huey Lewis would in later years - That it really is "hip" to be "square."

So, what was a singer-turned-actor to do when movie companies weren't making musicals or singing movies anymore?

"I soon began to realize that I had to turn things back over to the Lord," Boone said. "After all, He had opened all those doors for me in the first place. He could open them again."

And open them He did! Boone's spiritual rebirth was well chronicled in his book *A New Song,* which became a best seller. As his girls got older, Pat began to take the whole family on the road with him. Gradually, the Boone family was booking concert dates all over the country. People seemed to enjoy Pat Boone for who he was and the values that he and his wife Shirley stood for.

In recent years, Boone has been trying to slow things down a bit and spend more time with his grandchildren. His four daughters are all grown now, with kids of their own.

"Shirley and I married at 19, moved to Texas and I enrolled in North Texas State University," Pat said. "I was planning on being a preacher/teacher. I was going to teach English during the week and then preach on Sunday like a lot of preacher/teacher role models. I wanted to have an influence on young people and wanted to be the guy standing in the fork of the road saying 'Go this way' and 'Don't go that way.' 'Take this path because it leads to happiness and success and longevity and satisfaction. The other way leads to confusion, disappointment, disillusionment and finally death.'"

Certainly not all of his decisions have been perfect but, for the most part, Boone is a man who has chosen wisely. He has always made it a point to put God first and, because of that, he has been blessed beyond measure.

"God knew my heart," Boone said. "And because I tried to seek out the Lord's will in almost every decision that I made, He blessed me. He fulfilled all of my hopes and dreams of being an entertainer and I'm thankful that he was able to use me in that way."

Pat Boone was willing and God was certainly more than able.

"Young people and adults, too, should always be encouraged to aim high," Boone said. "They should dare to imagine, pray for and work towards high and almost unachievable goals. If you shoot high, even if you don't quite get to where you are aiming, you will probably get farther than if you just set mundane and ordinary goals for yourself. So I think it's important to at least dream and hope and pray for a significant thing, much like Abe Lincoln did."

Abraham Lincoln has long been one of Boone's heroes. Oddly enough, Boone may be related to the former U.S. president.

"I've been reading a book about Lincoln recently called *The Boones And The Lincolns* and how they were related," Boone said. "It is quite possible, according to the author of this book, that I might be related not only to Daniel Boone, but also to Abe Lincoln because there was some intermarriage between the two families. The thing about Lincoln is that there is no way, with his background and his beginnings, that he could have ever gone as far as he went. Or Will Rogers, the guy I'm playing out here in Branson. He was a Cherokee Indian, which was a definite minority in his day, and people put him in the second-class citizen category. Yet, he just kept plowing ahead and just kept liking people and kept doing what he could do, which was spin a rope and entertain people and make them laugh and that made him a celebrity. Lincoln's desire to become a good lawyer and then a judge eventually led him to the presidency."

Boone added that one of the keys to becoming successful is staying away from the negatives in life and, instead, focusing on some of the positives.

"In one of my books in the 1970s, I made an off-hand reference as to how distasteful some of the TV programming was at that time," he said. "But it's even worse now and there's no telling where it's going. With private or cable TV virtually unregulated, networks can get away with anything and they are. Orwell's *1984* may have been off a decade but what he promised or foretold is not really farfetched at all. The moral guidelines have become so blurred that the rule of the day seems to be that if you want to do something, you should be able to do it, unless you are actually killing somebody."

Those comments, however, are about as negative as Boone gets.

"Being negative is not the answer. I just try to be positive and point people toward positive role models. People have told me that I am a role model and I really try to be, although I'm sure I fall short a great deal of the time.

"I have four daughters and 15 grandchildren and I asked my oldest grandson if he remembers some of the things that I taught him when he was little. And he said 'I sure do.' And I asked him what they were and he said: 'God loves me, my parents and grandparents love me and I'm a good boy.'

"I've tried to teach him and the rest of my grandchildren that God loves them. That they are loved by their Creator. And that they are loved by their parents and grandparents no matter what. Hopefully, if they grow up that way, they are not going to stray too far from the kind of behavior that makes people really good. So, I can see that operating in their lives and, of course, Shirley and I have been trying to exemplify that to them, too. Of course, nobody is perfect and we certainly aren't, but if you shoot high and expect the best of yourself then the chances are good that most of the time you are going to achieve the goals you set for yourself."

Many have paid tribute to Boone over the years. He's had several gold albums, a star with his name on it on Hollywood Boulevard and many other outstanding awards and honors over his long career. But he said one of the most touching tributes he's ever had came from Sam Butcher, founder of "Special Moments" figurines.

"The figure is called 'Love Letters In The Sand' after a song I used to sing," Boone said. "It's a little boy drawing a heart-shaped letter in the sand and there's a little turtle looking over his hand as he is doing it. The letter in the inside of the heart simply says 'God Loves You.' I told Sam, and I was very emotional about it, that I hoped that he had summed up my life because, if this could truly be said of me and this was all that was ever said of me, then I would have achieved my highest goals in life and that my life was spent some way or another telling people that God loves them. And that is a very positive message. In fact that's what they call the Good News, The Gospel of Jesus Christ."

Not a bad lesson from a guy who has proven that it's "hip" to be "square."

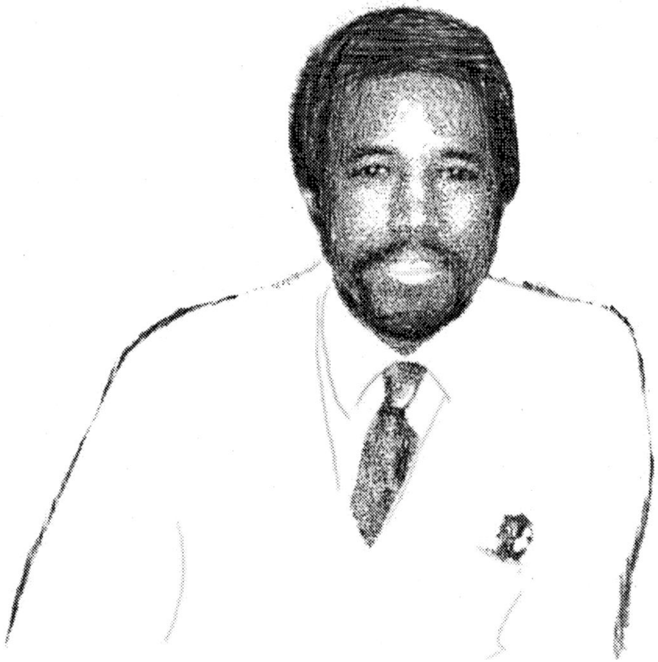

Dr. Ben Carson

The End of a Terrible Temper

Dr. Ben Carson is easily the most brilliant neurosurgeon of his time. When he became the first surgeon to successfully separate Siamese twins that were joined at the skull in 1987, he became a celebrity in his own right and soon the national talk shows and news programs were begging him to come on their programs. Yet Carson turned most of them down because he felt like it was inappropriate to be too self-serving. Besides, he's quick to add, it was God who should get the glory, not him. We met Dr. Carson at Johns Hopkins Hospital in Baltimore in the spring of 1993 and found him to be an interesting study of both charisma and humility. Today, he is one of the most renowned neurosurgeons in the world. But as a boy, he had much to overcome, including a violent temper. The story below was written in 1993, shortly after our visit with Dr. Carson. To read more of the inspiring story of Dr. Carson in his own words, we recommend his autobiography Gifted Hands: The Ben Carson Story.

Ben Carson had every excuse in the world not to be successful. But he refused to use them. His father had left Carson, his mother and his brother in poverty to fend for themselves. He and his brother were frequently sent away to live with relatives while his mother tried to make ends meet. He was a young African-American who grew up in the 1950s and 1960s when racism was strong in America.

Yet, for all his problems, he never complained. He went to work and did something about them.

While many of Carson's problems were beyond his control, there were several things that he realized that he could control. One of those was his violent temper.

One day after classes were out at Carson's high school in Detroit, he and his friend Bob were listening to the radio while walking home.

Bob didn't like the station that they were listening to and changed the dial. Soon the boys were in an argument, and in a moment of blind anger, Ben pulled a camping knife out of his back pocket and stabbed Bob just below the stomach with the knife.

Fortunately, the blade of the knife hit Bob's belt buckle and broke, sending the two boys off in opposite directions.

"When I think back on that time when I lost my temper and tried to stab my friend, I can't help but praise God that that boy wasn't hurt," Carson said during a 1993 interview. "We were walking home from school, listening to the radio. He changed the station and I got angry. I stabbed him with my camping knife but, fortunately, he had on a big belt buckle and the knife just broke off. He was so scared that he just ran off. I was scared, too."

A few days earlier, Carson had almost hit his mother after an argument over the kind of clothes he was to wear. Before that, he had thrown a rock at a boy and had broken the boy's glasses. That same year, Ben had hit another boy in the face with his fist while holding a combination lock.

All of these thoughts flooded Ben's mind as he raced home and locked himself in the bathroom shortly after trying to stab his friend. He knelt down beside the bathtub and asked the Lord to take away his terrible temper.

For several months Ben had tried to control his temper doing things his way. Now, he was turning it over to the Lord.

"It was one of the most amazing things that I have ever experienced," Carson said. "I have read a lot of psychology books on human behavior and all of them are quick to point out that temper is a personality trait and personality traits are not that easily changed. In fact, some psychologists say that personality traits are impossible to change. But God changed me that day in a miraculous way. I can honestly say that I haven't had a problem with my temper since that day."

At some point during his time of despair, Ben had slipped out of the small bathroom and had returned with a Bible. Almost immediately, his fingers had taken him to the pages of Proverbs, where he read verses about angry people and how their temper gets them into trouble.

"The verse that impressed me most that day was Proverbs 16:32," Carson said. "It says, 'He who is slow to anger is better than the mighty and he who rules his spirit [is better] than he who takes a city.'" (RSV)

From that day forward, Ben Carson was a new man. God had taken his terrible temper away from him and now God could use him to perform even more miracles.

Carson went on to graduate with honors from high school and continued his education at Yale University, where he was a pre-med major. From there, he went on to the University of Michigan to medical school. After years of medical school and long hours of working as an intern at Johns Hopkins University in Baltimore, Ben's dream of becoming a doctor had finally come true.

In the years ahead, Ben would find that his temper was just one of many obstacles he would encounter on his way to becoming one of the world's top neurosurgeons.

One of Carson's most successful surgeries came on Sept. 5, 1987 when he separated Siamese twins after 22 hours of surgery. Siamese twins occur only once in 70,000 to 100,000 births. Twins joined at the head are born once in every million births.

Yet, of all the surgeons in the world, it was Ben Carson, the man who had every excuse in the world to fail, who successfully separated them.

After several weeks of recovery, the two boys soon began to crawl around like two normal toddlers. Now [1993], both are healthy and happy and are in elementary school.

"When I think of all the things that God has allowed me to do, it is very humbling," Carson said. "He has enabled me to do some incredible things so that His name might be praised."

A couple of years ago, Carson was reminded of what might have been.

"In February of 1991, I was out at San Quinton Prison and was looking into those faces of the people who were in there," Carson said. "I realized then, that, had it not been for God and that belt buckle, I would have gone to jail or reform school and my life would have taken a decidedly different turn. I think it just goes to show you how much God loves us."

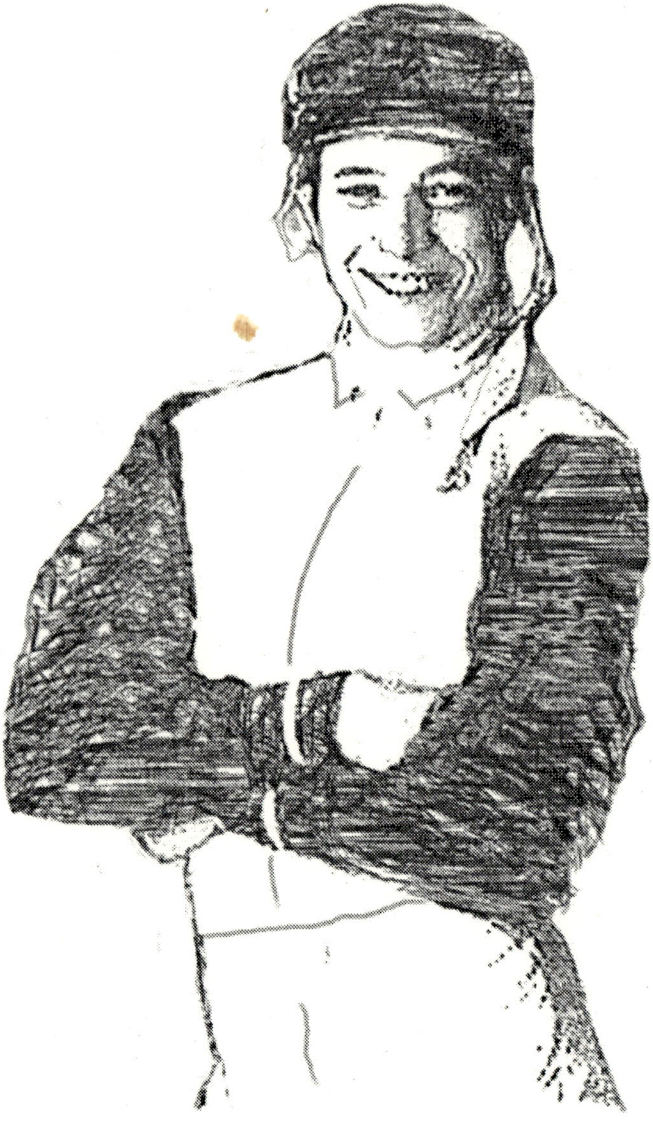

Steve Cauthen

The Kid From Walton

You didn't have to be a horse racing fan in the 1970s to know that Steve Cauthen was The Man. Every sports magazine you picked up in 1978 seemed to have him on the cover of it. Has it really been more than 25 years since "The Kid" was taking a shot at horse racing's Triple Crown? Somehow, it seems like only yesterday. It also seems like only yesterday when we visited with him, yet the story that appears below was written in the early 1990s. How did it feel to ride a horse to victory in all three legs of the Triple Crown? Probably not too bad at all, considering that Cauthen was not the jockey who was originally scheduled to ride a horse named Affirmed in the first place.

For the better part of the year, it had come down to a nose, a neck and a determined teenager.

In any other year, either horse might have been a Triple Crown Winner. But 1978 was not just any other year in the world of horse racing. It was the year of Affirmed and Alydar, considered by many racing experts to be one of the most incredible rivalries in horse racing history.

And, at the center of this two-horse rivalry was "The Kid," the boy who had barely turned 16.

Steve Cauthen well understood the path set before him. Winning the Triple Crown – the Kentucky Derby, Maryland's Preakness and New York's Belmont Stakes - is one of the most difficult accomplishments in all of sports.

Cauthen had prepared well for this grueling five-week stretch in which the three races were held. He had been riding horses since he was two-years-old. And had destroyed hundreds of bales of hay that he "rode" and whipped in the family's barn every day after school or whenever he could get the chance. There was 4-H, where he learned about grooming and showing horses and, more importantly, about the value of hard work. For as long as anyone at the Cauthen household could remember, Steve had never wanted to do anything else but become a jockey.

For novice racing fans, however, it might have seemed that Cauthen was an over-night success story. But for those who knew his family and had watched young Cauthen study other jockeys and ask questions while visiting racetracks near his home in Kentucky, this was certainly no "overnight" success. He had worked hard for a long time.

To understand the difficulty of winning the Triple Crown, one must consider this - that before Affirmed and Alydar matched speed and strength in their historic march to capture the Triple Crown in 1978, there had been only 10 other horses in the history of racing to accomplish this feat. In fact, prior to Seattle Slew's Triple Crown win in 1977, it had been more than 30 years since any horse had achieved the sport's highest honor.

So it was understandable that, as both Affirmed and archrival Alydar headed into the first race of the Triple Crown, the horses, owners and trainers were all having visions of winning it all.

As the Kentucky Derby began to get under way that Saturday in May of 1978, the crowd of 130,000-plus that had packed Churchill Downs expected a showdown between Affirmed and Alydar. In the end, racing fans would get all that they had bargained for.

Early in the race, a horse named Sensitive Prince raced from the far outside to gain the lead as the 11 horses completed the first half mile. Shortly after that, however, Affirmed and Cauthen steadily moved into the lead, jockeying with Believe It for first place. Between the top of the stretch and the eighth pole, Affirmed pulled away from Believe It and then, holding his own, waited for the challenge from Alydar.

"I hit my horse a few times as he drew away from Believe It," Cauthen told Pete Axthelm in his biography *The Kid.* "Then I started hand-riding him again, just trying to keep his mind on his business so he could take off again if Alydar came alongside him. And I kept looking back for Alydar."

Alydar had been accelerating gradually throughout the race. His jockey, Jorge Velasquez, laid low during most of the race, staying just behind the pace of Affirmed and Believe It. Suddenly, however, as expected, Alydar's devil's-red silks came into view as the horse accelerated dramatically down the home stretch, moving up from fourth place. Fans were on their feet as Alydar moved into second place and charged in a furious attempt to catch Affirmed.

In the end, Affirmed managed to hold off Alydar's dramatics and win the race by a narrow margin.

But, still, the close finish seemed to fuel the fire of the rivalry as the two horses headed into the second jewel of the Triple Crown, the Preakness in Maryland.

Alydar's trainer, John Veitch, said that, in this race, Cauthen and his mount would not get the jump on Alydar that they had gotten in the Kentucky Derby.

"Alydar is not going to spot Affirmed seventeen lengths like he did in Kentucky," Veitch told Axthelm. "I want him sharp enough to go after Affirmed early in the Preakness if he has to."

And go after him he did!

Going down the backstretch, Alydar was in next-to-last place. But, true to form, he began to accelerate with a burst of speed that held the promise of passing Affirmed and winning the race.

Cauthen, still in the lead, was not ready to concede his horse's position and whipped Affirmed hard with his right hand. Affirmed responded and, as the two horses neared the wire, it seemed to be either horse's race to win. The two champions ran the final 3/16ths of the race as fast as any two horses in the history of the Preakness. But Affirmed won by a nose.

Affirmed and Cauthen, two. Alydar and Velasquez, zero.

Now, only the Belmont Stakes stood in the way of the illusive Triple Crown.

As the race wound down at New York's Belmont Park, it appeared that Alydar might steal this third and last jewel of the Triple Crown. Affirmed had bolted from the gate and had taken an early lead, but after the first three quarters, Alydar had made his move and was at Affirmed's neck.

Cauthen and Affirmed. Velasquez and Alydar. Running almost neck-and-neck at an incredible pace that few observers thought could continue as they rounded the far turn.

But it did. Affirmed held his ground with Alydar making his characteristic sprint to the finish line.

In the end, however, it was merely the third verse of a sad song for fans of Alydar. Affirmed and The Kid had won again. This time only by a nose.

"The Preakness and the Belmont were probably two of the greatest races ever," said Cauthen, who is now retired. "When I look back at those old tapes of the race, I still get excited because they were just so close. It really just doesn't get any better than that. It's like Joe Montana hitting somebody in the end zone in the final seconds to win the game. It was just incredible."

"Incredible" was just one of the words that described it. "Heart-stopping" or "gut-wrenching" might be another description. For the jockey, trainer and owner of Alydar, it was simply frustrating. In any other year, Alydar might well have taken the Triple Crown himself.

"Alydar had actually pulled up even with me at one point in the Belmont," Cauthen said, recalling the race with a smile in his voice. "But I switched sticks and managed to get back in front. At the top level, jockeys switch sticks all the time. But, to me, that was the most crucial part of us winning the Belmont. At that point down the stretch, I knew it was time for me to dig deep and ask for something extra. I had never hit Affirmed left-handed before because I never really needed to. But that was the time. I realized that something had to be done and, fortunately, that got the required result. That helped spur him on and win the race."

The Triple Crown! A few strides either way and it could have been Alydar in the winner's circle. Cauthen, born on the day of the Kentucky Derby in May of 1960, reveled in the great two-horse rivalry.

"The whole rivalry seemed to capture the imagination of the public," Cauthen said. "Part of it was because it was such a great rivalry and part of it was because I was so young. It was an exciting time for me and an exciting time for racing. It really brought our sport to the forefront."

But the fortuitous teaming of Cauthen and Affirmed almost never happened.

"I had gone to New York in November of 1976 and the following year, 1977, really turned out to be a good year for me," Cauthen said. "I took a bad fall in May of 1977 and, while I was out, Affirmed had won his first two races. He won both of those races with Angel Corderro riding him. Then he went out to California and Lafitte Pinqua rode him. So, when you think about it, two of the greatest jockeys in the history of horse racing got a chance to ride him before I did."

Since Corderro had ridden Affirmed to two straight wins, he was the logical choice to ride him at a race scheduled for Saratoga in August of 1977. Oddly enough, however, Corderro had picked another horse to ride in the race and Pinqua was in California.

"Angel was offered the mount but had decided instead to ride a horse called Tilt Up," Cauthen said. "And Lafitte didn't want to fly all the way back from California to Saratoga to ride in such a small race. So they needed a jockey and I got the mount. I won that race and then continued to win on him and kept the mount."

So many outstanding jockeys never get the chance to prove themselves and Cauthen was certain that he was going to make the most of this opportunity.

"There are just so many things that go into being successful," Cauthen said. "I was very fortunate in that my family was in racing and that they encouraged me in what I wanted to do. Secondly, you have to be fortunate enough to get on a good horse and get the chance to compete in some of these big races. There are a lot of good jockeys that have never quite been lucky enough to get on a horse that is good enough to bring him into the limelight. Fortunately, I just happened to be at the right place, at the right time, on the right horse.

"There's only been 11 Triple Crown winners and Eddie Arcarro won two of them," Cauthen said. "It's a tough thing to do. The main requirement is that you have to have a horse that is capable, then you need quite a bit of good fortune along with it because there are so many things that could happen. You could lose just one of those three races by a nose and you've lost the Triple Crown. I think that's the great thing about my Triple Crown, which was the last one. At the time, there were some very good horses - Secretariat, Seattle Slew and Affirmed - and everyone seemed to think that it was getting easy. But it wasn't that, it was just that they were three great horses."

Shortly after his Triple Crown victory, Cauthen hit a slump. For 110 straight races, he failed to gain a single victory.

"It was something that was very difficult to explain," Cauthen said. "I was still working just as hard as I ever did, except that, this time, I wasn't winning. It was extremely frustrating, but my family and friends stood by me and, eventually, I worked my way out of it. But there was no doubt that it was a difficult time and I felt like I just needed a change of pace."

That change of pace proved to be a different continent. Shortly after Cauthen's streak of 110 consecutive losses had ended, he was offered the chance to ride in England. He was intrigued with the possibilities.

"Really, I was a success here in the United States for most of my career except for one month," Cauthen said. "Throughout my whole 14-year career in Europe, I was a success the whole time. I rebuilt my career over there. One of the reasons I went over there was because of my increasing weight and because of the fact that the weights over there were suited to heavier jockeys.

"And, to be quite honest, the losing streak was a tough time. I never thought of quitting or doing anything else, though. I had won some races after losing 110 straight and had started working to get back on top when this offer from Europe came. It just seemed like the right thing for me to do. I was never trying to run away from anything or anything like that."

It was a move that paid off handsomely for young Cauthen. He got out of the spotlight of the United States and into the limelight of The Old Country.

"Frankly, the pressure of being the center of attention for nearly three years in America, which I was, begins to wear on you after a while. Over there [in Europe], I was still the center of attention in many ways but the pace of life was a little slower over there and the whole change seemed to suit me really well. People accepted me and that was nice, too."

When you are a young man with Cauthen's personality and charm it is easy to be liked. As he steadily won more than 1,800 races in Europe, he also found himself accepted by the European horse racing community.

"It was another challenge," he said. "A new challenge. And I think it was a pretty good accomplishment to win over there because the courses are different and the style is different. Going over there and re-adapting to a totally new course and style was difficult. I feel good about my accomplishments over there.

"I had done most of the things that you could do. Not that I didn't want to continue to ride Triple Crown winners. But the problem was that I could see that, in the long run, it was going to be difficult for me to maintain my weight to the level that was required in U.S. horse racing. That had a lot to do with me deciding to go to Europe."

No jockey had won more races than Steve Cauthen from 1976 until his Triple Crown win in 1978. While some observers speculated that there were no more mountains to conquer for young Cauthen, it was more a question of weight than it was new goals or challenges.

"Sure, there were other races that I would have wanted to win," he said. "There were times when I would come back from Europe to visit and would think about winning the Breeder's Cup and other races like that. But the problem wasn't the fact that I couldn't come back and win the odd race.

"The problem was my weight. To be successful in the U.S., a jockey needs to at least be able to get down to 115 and the best I could get down to was 119. It's only four pounds and it may not seem like a lot, but it means a lot to a jockey. Weight was a big factor in a lot of the decisions that I made."

For 14 years, Cauthen called England home. During that time, he won more than 1,800 races while riding at a more comfortable weight. He was also riding in fewer races, which was a nice change of pace from the hectic work schedule of a jockey in the United States.

"They don't have as much racing over there as we do in the U.S.," Cauthen said. "Their racing is seasonal and they only race on the flat from March until November. There are only six races a day on a given race card."

The champion jockey in England, Cauthen noted, would ride somewhere between 150 and 175 horses a year on the average.

"But even though they don't have as many races as we do in the U.S., it was extremely competitive," he said. "I really liked the variety and the different courses. They have right-handed courses, left-handed courses and they also have a Figure Eight course in England. It was interesting and challenging and all of the racing was on turf. There was just a lot of history behind the racing in England and it was just a great experience."

For the most part, going to England was an extremely positive experience for Cauthen. A few years after he got over there, however, he began to realize that he had a problem with alcohol.

"Along the way, I did have my problems with alcohol," Cauthen said in a straightforward tone. "But alcohol, drugs and all of those things take a person backwards and I don't want to go backwards. When you start to see yourself drifting away, you need to get back to the things that make you successful."

In 1985, Cauthen said, he found that he was starting to "drift away."

"It was in 1985 while I was in still in Europe," Cauthen said. "I had been in Europe for six years and it was a few months into 1985 when I decided that I just didn't want to drink anymore. It had never really affected my riding. I still raced and did the things that I normally did. But I began to realize that there was a possibility that it could have a very negative effect on me and I realized that I just had to stop."

Cauthen's constant battle with weight also played a part in his bout with alcohol, he said.

"I started to drink more as a result of my weight struggles because I just wasn't happy with myself and my weight," Cauthen said. "So I guess I started to drink more as a way to make me feel better or whatever. But, in the end, it really didn't make me feel better and, in fact, it was taking me further and further from my goals.

"A lot of it was peer pressure, the pressure of everyday life. Maybe it was the fact that it was 'socializing,' I don't know.

"It's easy to get into something and suddenly find that you're in over your head. But, luckily, you have friends that try to warn you before you get in too deep. Then again, you never know. It's a deep down thing that you probably realize before you ever do anything about it or make the move.

"I did go through some counseling. It was difficult because you don't want to accept that there is something wrong with you or that you can't handle something or whatever. But it was time to let go of it and get on with my life."

And that's exactly what Cauthen did as he had several more years of success in England. Things were also getting better in his personal life. It was in England that he met a girl named Amy, who would later become his wife.

"Amy and I grew up about 20 miles from each other in Kentucky but we met in England," Cauthen said. "She was over there as part of her studies for college. When people ask where we're from and we tell them, they naturally think that we met here in Kentucky, but that wasn't the case at all. Maybe it was just fate."

In August of 1994, Cauthen became one of the youngest, if not the youngest, jockey ever to be inducted into The

National Racing Hall of Fame in New York. At 34, he had accomplished more than a lot of jockeys twice his age.

Cauthen, who used to spend hours upon hours studying films of races, says he now enjoys helping others learn about the sport.

"Horse racing can still be exciting, even if you don't know a lot about it," he said. "But when you start to learn about some of the subtleties that go into it, it really becomes exciting because you can start to comprehend what's really happening and you can start to see what is going through the mind of some of the jockeys in the race.

"You see a situation where a guy has been outmaneuvered or has made a great technical move and it has made the difference in him winning or losing. And that's what's wonderful about the sport. Knowledge is important to appreciation. One of my goals is to better explain our sport so that more people can enjoy it and appreciate it.

"I was a kid from a small town and, basically, I just wanted to stay that way," Cauthen said. "I never wanted to change my personality just because I was successful and I tried to always stick to that. I always want to treat people decently. Success is one thing, but the most important thing is to be a decent person."

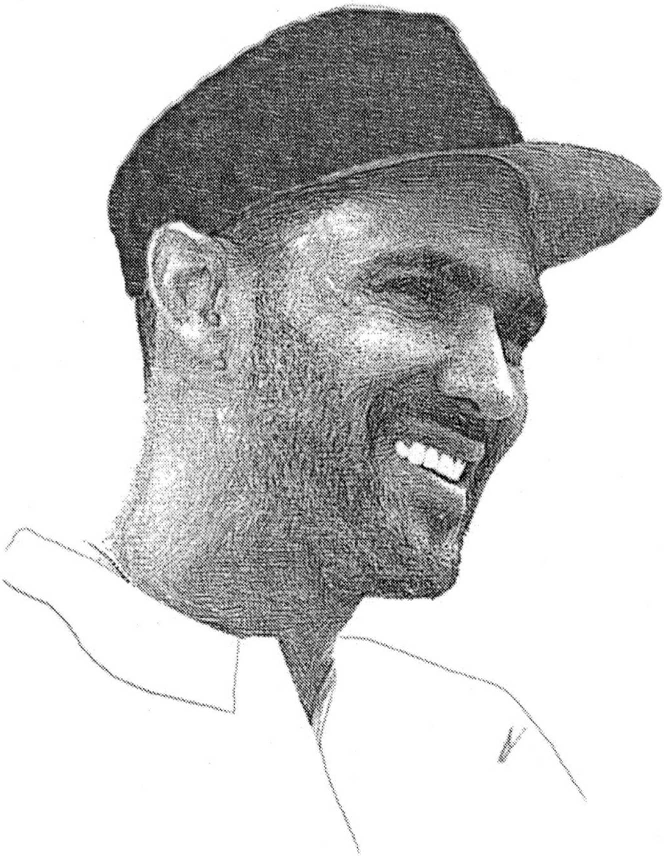

Tony Dungy

Heart of a Champion

Shortly after we heard Indianapolis Colts Head Coach Tony Dungy speak at Oak Cliff Bible Fellowship in Dallas in the spring of 2004, we knew we had to include him in this book. Sometimes, the best thing a writer can do is to get out of the way and just let the subject tell the story. Below is just a slightly edited version of the speech Tony gave at a men's breakfast at Oak Cliff Bible Fellowship on March 27, 2004. Special thanks to Tony Dungy for letting us use the text of his speech in this book and also to Pastor Tony Evans, pastor of Oak Cliff Bible Fellowship, for inviting us to hear such an incredible man of God share the Gospel of Christ and inspire us to live for the Lord.

"As I thought about what I wanted to talk about today, I thought about what Jesus did in these type of settings. When he was around large crowds of people and he would have to share important things with them in a short amount of time, He would always use parables to make His point. He would talk about things that people were familiar with and then He would apply those points to the Kingdom of God. So I wanted to do that today and I thought: What do I know about that a thousand men in Texas might understand? I'm not real smart but it occurred to me that I could talk a little football and you guys might get a better feel for my message today.

"So we're going to take some things from football and then apply them to the Kingdom of God.

"As most of you may know, two years ago I left Tampa Bay and I was looking for employment and was interviewing with some owners around the NFL. All ownership is pretty much the same. They all have this goal of going to the Super Bowl and they want to know how you are going to help them do that. So I sat down with the Colts ownership up in Indy and we talked about how we were going to bring a Super Bowl to the Colts if I came there.

"But more than that, I wanted to make sure that they understood that my plan was to get us to the Super Bowl, but if it was only that, only success on the field, it was going to be very short-lived and it wasn't going to be worth very much. I wanted to make it clear that we wanted to do it with the right kind of people, the right type of atmosphere to win but I also wanted a team that would make a difference in Indianapolis. And I think the process is coming along.

"In 2002, we made a lot of progress towards that. This past year [2003], we were very close to winning it all. And people always ask us, when was the defining moment? And the defining moment for us wasn't even really a game. It wasn't even on the practice field. The defining moment for us was in a chapel service. We have a 30-minute chapel service before the games and we had a speaker that came in and talked about the heart of a champion. And he hit it so perfectly that our guys remembered it and talked about it all season. I started talking about it. It became kind of a rallying cry for our team and any time we are in a tough situation, guys would just say 'Hey, do we have the heart of a champion or not?' And it became such a big thing that our whole team picked up on it. As a matter of fact, our highlight film that will be coming out this year [2004] that describes this past season is titled 'Heart of a Champion.'

"The speaker made five points. He took each letter of the word 'Champ' and made a point out of each letter. Then he talked about what you really have to do to be a winner. He started out this way:

"*C.* If you want to be a champion, or champ, that word starts with a *C* and *C* stands for Commitment. You have to be committed. But before you can be committed, you have to really be convinced about a topic you believe in. That's my job as the head coach. I've got to set the goals. I have to ask myself 'Where do we want to go?' I've got to give the team direction, and more importantly, talk about how we're going to get there.

"In football, you can do it a lot of different ways. In Tampa, we were a defensive team. In Indianapolis, we're an offensive team. You can be flashy; you can be conservative. You can take chances; you can gamble. You can play it close to the vest. There are a lot of ways to do it, but everybody has to believe in it and everybody has to be committed to it in order for it to work. My job as a head coach is to pick the team the proper way so that we get guys who really believe in what we're doing. I also have to set the practice schedule. We can work on situations and we can put ourselves in positions of what we are going to see in the game and what our weaknesses are. We can work on all those things.

"I give the motivational talks. I'm going to do everything I can to get those 53 guys to share the vision that I have of how we're going to get to the Super Bowl.

"The player's job, conversely, is to buy into what I'm saying. To really, really believe it. To sell out 100 percent to it. And that sounds real easy. But that's the biggest challenge in athletics. To get guys to buy in. A championship team doesn't need a bunch of all-stars. It doesn't need the most talented guys. And that's what I tell our guys all the time. I'm not going to pick the 53 best players to be on this team. I'm going to pick the 53 guys who really buy in and believe in what we're doing and where we're going.

"You would think that everybody does that and that everybody wants to win. Well, everybody plays hard and everybody does give 100 percent. But that's not what winning a championship is all about. You hear of players who won't come off the bench to help their team and don't do the things that their coaches ask them to do to make the team successful. You look for players who will be committed to the team and who will buy into what you're talking about. And we have to sell that all the time.

"If you ask every player in the National Football League if they want to win a championship, all 1600 of them would tell you 'yes.' No question about it. You can count on me, Coach. Then when you go a little bit deeper and say, okay, this is what I need you to do: you're going to be a receiver for me and we're going to win a Super Bowl but you're not going to catch a single pass. Suddenly, I'll hear 'Coach, I've got to think about that one.'

"Or another one that we have to say sometimes is: 'Hey, we need you. We need your leadership. You're going to help us win a Super Bowl, but because of where we are in the salary cap, I can only afford to pay you the minimum salary.

Then you hear 'Man, you just disrespected me, Coach. I want to win but it's not about all that. You've got to take care of me.'

"It's a tough, tough thing when you talk about that total commitment and buying into the program. But if we can get that total commitment, that's really the first step. And then we're going in the right direction.

"Now, once you get that commitment and if you can get it from 53 guys, you're on your way. But, if you ever do get that type of commitment, challenges are going to come. So that leads to the second part of the equation. The second letter in the word 'Champ' is *H*. And that is *H* as in 'Handling adversity.' How are you going to handle things when adversity comes? No one goes undefeated. Even the best teams in the league stumble here and there. How are you going to get back up and stay on course when things don't go exactly as you plan them? Handling adversity is big in the NFL and I think the first thing you have to do is really understand what adversity is.

"Many times, we really don't understand. As players, as coaches and even as Christians we don't understand what adversity is. The Bible talks about it in John 16:33 where it says that 'In this world you will have tribulation.' So we expect it to come but we don't always understand what it is and what it isn't. The first thing you have to do is recognize what it is not.

"One of my favorite coaches of all time was a guy named Al McGuire. Most of you may know him as an announcer today but he was a great coach and he was a neat guy. When I was in high school, his team, Marquette, was playing South Carolina and there was a big fight in the game.

"Usually, basketball fights aren't really much of anything. But these guys were really fighting and it took them about

10 minutes to clear the floor and they finally got the game played. After the game, they asked McGuire about it and the reporters were saying how terrible it was to have that type of fight on national TV. McGuire just shrugged and said, 'I wouldn't call that a fight, I thought it was more of a discussion. I'm from New York and I grew up in a bar that my father owned. We never called it a fight until the bouncer took his jacket off and the bouncer would have handled that one without even taking his coat off.'

"McGuire was making the point that it really wasn't that tough and that's what I tell my team all the time - that these situations are really not that tough. We get into these situations that seem tough, like when we were down by 21 points at halftime in a game against Tampa on Monday Night Football during the 2003 season and it really wasn't that tough. The bouncer really hasn't even taken his jacket off yet. This isn't that bad. We can get this done. And that's what we have to understand.

"To really understand what tribulation is, we need to go to Hebrews 11:36 and remember the part where it reminds us that some Christians faced jeers and floggings while still others were chained and put in prison. They were stoned. They were sawed in two. They were put to death by the sword. They went about in sheepskins and goatskins, destitute, persecuted and mistreated. THAT'S adversity okay?

"So when people come up to me and say, 'Oh, man, they fired you. You went to the playoffs for three years in a row and they fired you. How did you handle such great adversity?' That wasn't adversity. What those early Christians went through, THAT was adversity. People talk about me being calm on the sidelines but it's only because I understand what adversity is. When they start sawing me in half and I'm still that calm, then you'll know I've got it. Losing two games in a row is not adversity. I can't help but laugh at Christians sometimes when I hear them say things like 'Oh, my car broke down and I've got to take the bus for a week. But God said that there would be adversity and I've got to handle it.' That is NOT adversity. So we have to get that straight.

"But there are times when real adversity comes. If Payton Manning gets hurt in the first game and is out for the season, then THAT'S some adversity right there.

[Laughter]

"When we get to that, we have to handle it.

"So how do you handle that real adversity when it comes? Those really, really tough situations? That's where commitment comes in. In I Corinthians 15:58 it says, 'Stand firm. Be unmovable.' That's how you deal with real adversity when it comes. My first coach, the guy I learned all my professional football from, Chuck Knoll, he was great that way. When things would come up and the media would start getting on him, he would tell them that the Pittsburgh Steelers were not going to change. 'We have a system. We have a Steeler way of doing things and we are going to do it that way,' he told them. They'd get mad at him, say that the game has passed him by and call him stubborn. Knoll would just look at them and say, 'You know what? Stubbornness is a virtue when you are right. It's only a fault when you're wrong and I'm not going to be wrong very often.' So be unmovable. Be really committed to what you are all about. That's how you handle adversity.

"The next thing that that chapel speaker talked about was the *A* in the word 'Champ' and the *A* is for 'Attitude.' But before you can have the right attitude in sports, you have to have another *A* and that's accountability. Personal responsibility. We're seeing it all the time now in the NFL. Players want that status of being a star. They want the perks that go along with being a star. But they don't want all the responsibility. But, hey, it comes with the territory. We get guys all the time who say, 'Coach, I really don't want to live in town. I really don't want to work out in the off-season. You're cramping my style. Or, we'll try to sign them, and before we do, we'll have a conversation where I tell them that, hey, I want you on the team, but there are some other things that I want you to do. You have to be a role model. You have to be a leader. You've got to be the guy people look up to and you've got to stay out of trouble.

"And then I get, 'Coach, why do you want to put that on me. My personal business shouldn't have anything to do with what I do on the football field.' But I tell them that it does have something to do with it. And that if they are going to play for the Colts, then they have to be personally accountable.

"That's why I enjoying coaching a guy like Payton Manning. Manning is a great leader and sets a great example for the rest of the team. This is a guy who works hard. He watches film and has his own video lab in his basement so that he can watch tape after our meetings and he doesn't miss a practice. He doesn't miss a turn and does everything you ask and then, when you do lose a ball game, he stands up and says, 'I've got to play better next week for us to win.' That type of personal accountability is what you need if you are going to be a champion.

"You also need accountability in your Christian life. You can't just have the benefits of the Christian life and not accept the responsibility. I learned that in Pittsburgh when I went to the Steelers when I was 21 years old. I was very fortunate. I grew up in a home where my mom taught Sunday school, I learned the Gospel early and I accepted Christ. But I was like a lot of young guys back then and today. When I was 14 or 15 I just played ball all the time. Football was everything to me. I knew I was saved. I knew I was going to heaven. But my motivation was to have fun and play ball and go to school and just enjoy life.

"So I got to the NFL and I wasn't really growing and I wasn't really thinking about the Lord. I wasn't bad. But I was just having fun. I got there and I ran into about 10 guys who were completely different than anybody that I had ever been around. These guys were different. Their language was different. The way they treated their family was different. The way they treated everybody else was different. They were just unique, on-fire Christian guys.

"I started hanging out with these guys and I started going to the Bible studies and going to the chapels and what I understood from those guys was that it wasn't just a once a week thing or just going to church on Sundays. It was how you lived. It was accepting that responsibility that if Christ was in you, He had to be in charge every day – even on the field. And that's what turned me around. That's what made me realize that I had to be accountable every single day.

"Pastor Evans talked about it earlier today. And he didn't tell the whole story. He asked me if I had ever let a curse word slip out and I said, 'Well, not since I've been a head coach.' There were a couple of times when I was an assistant that some guys heard some things that they shouldn't have heard. But I understand that when I'm a head coach, that camera is always on me. And I have proclaimed to be a Christian and I don't want Christ to look bad because the camera is on me and I'm saying something that I shouldn't say.

"After accountability is Motivation. The *M* in the word 'Champ' is for 'Motivation' and that is extremely critical for us if we are going to build our team the right way. Why is a guy playing the game? And that's a critical question to ask because, if the motivation changes, many times the performance can change, too.

"We're spending a lot of time now looking at players because the draft is coming up next month and we're looking for guys to be a part of our Colts team and we'll test them. We'll time them and we'll measure them, weigh them and put them through all these athletic drills to see if they have the physical skills to play in the NFL.

"But more than that, I want to find out what motivates those guys because that is going to determine how well they play for us. There are a lot of things that motivate young players. Many times it's the idea of money. Many times it's acceptance, fame or notoriety. A lot of times it's the Super Bowl. They want to play for a team where they can win a championship. But if they are really just motivated by that, you aren't going to have lasting success with that player. If a player is only motivated by money and he signs and gets enough money to last him for the rest of his life before he even steps on the field and he's only motivated by money, then he's not going to perform real well for us.

"Notoriety? They are going to get that very quickly. Even the Super Bowl. You can see it. A team will strive so hard to get there. They'll talk about it, they'll get there and the next year, they'll have the same players but they can't get there because they've gotten there before and they've fulfilled that motivational desire and it's not the same.

"We have found that the guys who do the best are the guys who are really motivated by the challenge of the job. They want to do well every year, every game, every play because that's what the job entails and that's what they are supposed to do. They are motivated by being the best they can possibly be in every situation. If we can get those players, if we can get all of those elements in place, then we've got a chance to build a championship team.

"But the most important element in becoming a champion is the *P*, the last letter of the word 'Champ.' And *P* stands for being plugged into the right power source. Who are you relying on? And that's so important with a football team or an athletic team. You can have all those other factors in place – the commitment, the ability to handle adversity, the attitude, the motivation, but if they are listening to the wrong sources, it creates problems. If we are going to build a championship team, then they can only listen to the coaches and the veteran leadership on the team. If it's anything else, we're going to have problems. It can't be their agent. It can't be the media and it can't even be friends and family. In fact, a lot of times, friends and family members can be the worst. We have a section in our stadium that's called 113. It's right behind our bench. And you know who sits there – the wives and the girlfriends.

"You hear things like 'Why don't they block for my husband? Why don't they give my boyfriend the ball more? Why do they put *him* in there, he can't play!

"And all of that goes with the territory. But the players can't listen to that. That's why it's just so important to be plugged into the right power source.

"One point I'd like to make to the young guys in the audience. They often think that, man, if I could just make it to the NFL and play professional football, life couldn't be any better. Everything would be all right and I'm going to put everything into doing that.

"But I've got a little news for you. That's not necessarily the case. I was at the Super Bowl this year and there was an article in the local newspaper that kind of shocked me. I knew it to a certain extent but I couldn't believe it when I actually saw it in print. This reporter wrote about what actually happens to our players in the NFL after they finish playing the game. Did you know that 78 percent of NFL players, within one year after they retire, either file for bankruptcy, unemployment or divorce? I didn't believe it.

"I called our NFL office and told them that the guy who wrote that story was exaggerating. They shocked me by saying that it wasn't an exaggeration. In that Super Bowl that you watched a few months ago, there were 106 players on the field that day – 53 on each team. If they all retired today, chances are that, by this time next year, 80 of them would file for bankruptcy, unemployment or divorce. And that's hard to believe. But what it tells us is that football is not life.

"Football can characterize life. But it just happens faster. If you come into football at 21-years old, you're a baby in the NFL. At 25, you are middle age. At 29, you're a senior citizen. Things happen fast. The average life span of an NFL player is about 3.7 years. So after about six years, you've seen a lifetime of things. And what you have to understand is that it's not how you start but how you finish. That's what really tells the story of your life. You can have a great career and still wind up as one of those statistics. One of those 78 percent. So what you have to do is apply those championship principles that we were talking about and you have to apply them to how you live. That's what that chapel speaker was trying to say that day. That's what Jesus was trying to say in all of his parables. You've got to take these principles that I'm talking about and you have to apply them to what really matters. Don't just win games. Don't just have a successful business career and end up as one of those stats. It's how you finish that counts.

"If you only remember one thing that I say today, remember this: If you don't have a relationship with Christ, the end of the story is not going to be pretty. No matter how good things look now, no matter how you feel, no matter what type of status that you have, if you don't know Jesus Christ as your Savior, your story is not going to have a happy ending. You can be an all-pro in the NFL and have everything in the world going for you. But if you don't have that rock solid relationship with Christ, the movie is going to have a sad ending and you're going to be crying at the end. On the other hand, if you do have a relationship with Christ, you need to ask yourself how God can use you to become a part of that team.

"Just like a football team God, too, is trying to build a winning team and he doesn't need all-stars; He needs those people with the heart of a champion. The same things that we discussed earlier are the same things that are going to make a great team for Christ and eternity.

"You have to be convinced of the truth of the Gospel. You have to understand that Christ died for our sins and that He died not just to be our Savior but he also died so that he could be the center of our lives. And if you understand that, then you have to be committed to it. You have to be sold out to it. Regardless of the role that God wants you to play. We'd all like to be the quarterback. We'd all like to be the star. We'd all like to be the guy who gets all the attention. But God may just want you to come off the bench. And you can't say, 'That's not for me. I can't come off the bench.'

"You've got to say, 'If that's what you want, if that's what it's going to take to make us a winning team, then bring me off the bench because I'm convinced of your plan and your program.'

"You've also got to be a little steadfast and a little stubborn. Just like that verse in I Corinthians 15:58 says, stand firm and don't be moved, even when it's not popular. I know I've lost a lot of jobs that I've applied for because the owners asked me 'Is getting to the Super Bowl the most important thing in your life? Can I count on you being there 24 hours a day and being available around the clock to do whatever it takes to win a Super Bowl?' And my response was, 'No. No you can't. Because if that's what it takes to have this job, then I don't want it.' It's not popular. It's not always going to get you ahead. But I don't want anything to come before my relationship with Christ.

"That's the most important thing. Being plugged into the right power source. What's driving you? Where do you get your direction for life? Who do you listen to when you're making crucial, critical decisions? If you're not plugged into Christ, then you are going to end up with problems. If it's not the Bible that you're getting your direction from, then you'll go the wrong way. If it's not the Holy Spirit that you're listening to when you're making those critical decisions then you don't know if you're going to be right or wrong. And if you're not plugged into the right power source, even if you have everything else in life, then eventually you'll short circuit if you are not plugged into the right place.

"As it says in Matthew 16:26, 'What does it profit a man to gain the whole world and lose his soul?' And in 25 years of NFL football, believe me, I've seen that. I've seen some guys who have done everything that you can do from a football standpoint. From the world's standpoint. Gone to Super Bowls. Gone to Pro Bowls. Gotten inducted into the NFL Hall of Fame. Have made tons of money. And then lost everything.

"I would just urge you today to check your heart out. Are you plugged into Christ? Do you have the heart of a champion? If you do, continue to develop that. Continue to think that way because God is going to use you to build his championship team here on earth. If you aren't plugged into the right source, if you aren't plugged into Christ, then don't leave this auditorium today without doing that. Commit yourself to the Lord. Let Him handle your adversity for you. Let Him make you accountable. Let Him give you the motivation to be a champion so that you can end up the right way as a champion and not as a statistic. Thank you very much."

[Applause]

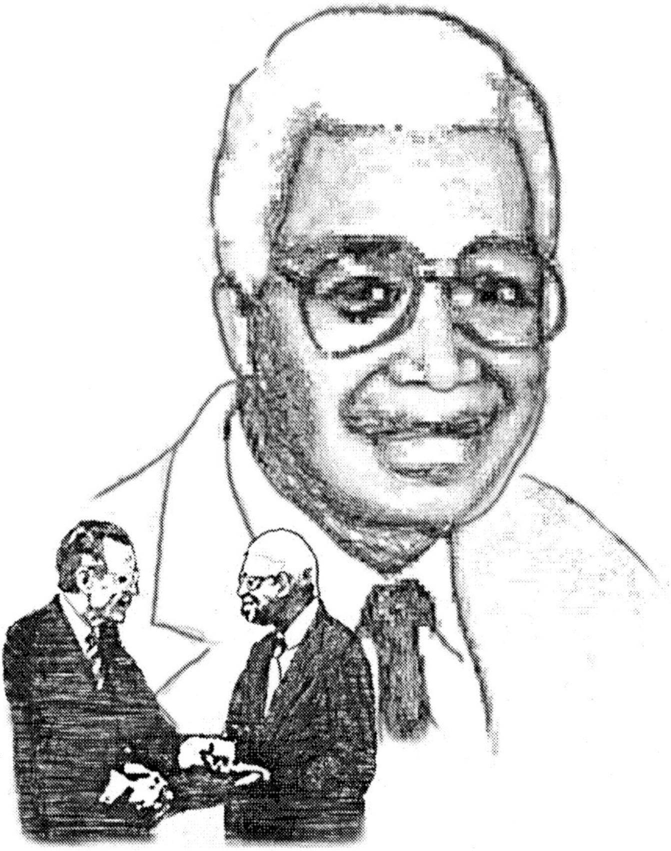

Thomas Fleming

Super Teacher

He was a high school dropout who couldn't even read until he was in the military, yet he went on to become a National Teacher of the Year. We met Thomas Fleming in Atlanta in 1993, and what we found was that he was always teaching someone something. Even when he wasn't in the classroom. The story that appears below was written in 1993.

The red light on Thomas Fleming's phone at the Westin Hotel in downtown Atlanta was blinking furiously, yet it wasn't ringing. A visitor had tried to reach the 1992 National Teacher of the Year earlier but, because of the defective ringer, Fleming wasn't getting the message.

After a bellboy's summons, the elevators in the main lobby open and Fleming emerges, somewhat disgruntled with the fact that none of his messages were getting through.

He greets his visitor politely and then marches straight to the hotel's front desk to address the problem.

"My phone is not working properly," he tells the clerk firmly but politely. "This gentleman here has been trying to get through to me for more than an hour and I haven't been able to hear the phone ring. I expect this problem to be corrected immediately."

The clerk assures him that the problem will be taken care of and Fleming and his visitor get on the elevator. On the way up, a woman recognizes him. She has come to Atlanta for the National Drop-out Convention, which Fleming will address later that evening.

"I'm looking forward to speaking to your group," Fleming said, smiling. "You know, I was a drop-out myself. Fortunately, though, I dropped back in."

He gives the woman one of his cards and she thanks him. Fleming is nothing if not a teacher. Even when he is not in the classroom, he is teaching. Showing how, with a lot of hard work and a desire to learn, you too can do anything you set your mind to do. He is a walking, talking example of how a teacher should conduct himself and, even if you did not know who he was or what he did for a living, it would be easy to guess his profession. Teacher, you would probably say to yourself, this guy's a teacher.

Once in his hotel room, Fleming offers his visitor a chair and briefly excuses himself to call the front desk.

"This is Mr. Fleming," he tells the clerk. "Is someone going to come up here and fix my telephone? Okay, thank you very much. Could you ring it for me? I'll hang up."

The phone rings. Fleming answers it, thanks the clerk again and hangs up.

"Sorry about that," he says. "You, my wife and other people have been trying to get through and this crazy phone has not been ringing. I think we've got it straightened out now, though."

Perhaps this minute attention to detail is what has made Fleming so successful in the teaching field. Teaching in both an era and an area where crime and violence in the public school system is at an all-time high, Fleming has seen a little bit of everything at Michigan's Washtenaw County Juvenile Detention Center in Ann Arbor, Michigan over the past 20 years. It is here that Fleming teaches history, government and geography in a one- room schoolhouse.

"It's important to realize that the kids that I work with are offenders, but they are not criminals," he said. "That's the key. When you use the word 'criminal' to describe a 12- or 13-year-old kid, that's not what we're dealing with. We're dealing with another 'C' and that's confusion. There is a tremendous sense of abandonment that leads to delinquency or it may be abuse where some adult has exploited a child. These kids are angry and, to a great extent, very distrustful. Once I became aware of that, I could work for their trust.

"Once those young people realized that I wasn't going to hurt them, that I wasn't going to abuse them, then those young people could begin to get back in touch with the youth of their life and the creative potential of their life."

His efforts over the past two decades have earned him education's highest honor - The 1992 National Teacher of the Year Award. The recipients of this award are chosen from all 50 states, five extra-state jurisdictions, the District of Columbia and the Department of Defense Dependent Schools. They are selected on the basis of nominations by students, teachers and school administrators. The award is sponsored by the Council of Chief State School Officers and Encyclopedia of Britannica, Inc.

"I certainly didn't plan it that way," he said. "You don't come from where I came from and want to be a teacher. But

I found that it was something that I enjoyed doing and I've just stayed with it."

As part of the National Teacher of the Year program, Fleming traveled the United States extensively in 1993 and also traveled to some different countries as well, encouraging young teachers as well as older ones.

"Many good teachers have left the profession and there are a number of reasons for that," he said. "What I like to tell young teachers is that, before you even start, be sure you have a passion for teaching because, if you don't, the paycheck will not keep you there and the 9 1/2 months of work with a nice summer off will not keep you there. You need to have a passion to work with young people and to be ready for the unpredictable."

"Unpredictable" is a good word to describe Fleming's career path, for few would have predicted that this boy who couldn't read and who dropped out of school at the age of 17 to join the national guard would inspire so many young people with his work in the classroom.

"For me, it has been a combination of many things," Fleming said. "I discovered a place that was mine and I discovered a population that I could relate to. These young people, in their search, had a journey that was very similar to mine. At one point in their lives, they turned off the educational experience. I did the same thing. I see kids every day who are so frustrated because they can't sort things out. I've been there.

"So much of the exchange I've had with them is one in which I tell them that there is a better alternative to all those negative things that they're doing. I say to young people all the time, 'Be pro-active, not re-active.' If you look at life from a pro-active standpoint, you will find solutions to a lot of the problems and obstacles you see in front of you."

Fleming is no stranger to obstacles and problems. He will be the first to tell you that he brought a lot of them on himself but, like many kids in the urban area of Detroit in the late 1950s, he was just looking for a way out.

"I was tired of going to school so I just dropped out," he said. "I was attending Chatsey Trade School in Detroit at that time and I left school at the age of 17 during a summer break. I told a lie to get into the National Guard and thought I was pretty cool."

President Harry S. Truman, however, decided to activate the National Guard and sent them to fight in the Korean War.

"When Truman activated the Guard, I quickly decided to tell the truth," Fleming recalled, flashing a broad smile. "But, at that point, it was just a little too late."

As it turned out, however, Fleming and his other underage friends (many of them had also lied about their age to get into the Guard) were deemed too young to participate in the Korean conflict. Still, Fleming related how uncomfortable he was when he learned about the possibility of going to Korea.

"Here I was scheduled to go to Korea and I couldn't even read," he said. "Even though I didn't officially drop out of school until I was 17, I tell people that I had mentally dropped out of school at age 13. It was just so frustrating to go to school and try to tackle reading, writing and arithmetic and just be in a fog. So, the things that kept me in school during this time lied in the change in my peer group."

When Fleming was 14, his family moved from a predominately white neighborhood in Detroit to a predominately black neighborhood on the west side of town.

"The new kids that I met on the west side began to accept me as one of the home boys," he said. "Even though the group that I hung out with was somewhat delinquent, I enjoyed being with them because they accepted me and I felt a part of their group."

It was through this peer group that Fleming was exposed to guns.

"One of my classmates had access to quite a few guns," he said. "I know he had a least two because he pointed two at me! One was a .45-caliber handgun and the second gun was a .22. I only remember what the second gun was because it went off when he was pointing at me. When it fired, it missed me and it hit one of my buddies, who was behind me. We had skipped school that day and we were over at his house, playing around and acting like we were going to shoot each other. So it was really just an accident that the gun went off. But, when it did, it really woke me up and it was at that point that I realized how close death was. I was about 15 or 16 when that happened and that really woke me up."

His friend survived the shooting but the experience left Fleming with a nagging sense of the hereafter. A few years later, while serving in the U.S. Army, Fleming was stationed in France when he broke the small cross that his mother had given him as a young boy.

"My mother told me that that cross had been blessed by a Catholic priest," Fleming said. "When I broke that cross while carrying it in my wallet, I thought I had damned my soul forever. I was very serious when I went to the chaplain and I was very upset. I think he thought I was some kind of wacko and he didn't know how to handle it. He sent me to another chaplain and he couldn't help me much, either."

Finally, Fleming found the help he needed in the motor pool where he worked.

"Back at the motor pool, I had a friend named David that was a truck driver," Fleming said. "I don't even remember his last name but I can remember having a long talk with him. He told me about Christ and I started going to a Bible study with him. It was through that group that I began to get a desire to learn how to read because I wanted to be able to read the book of Mark.

But Fleming knew that it wasn't going to be easy.

"At that time, I couldn't even read the military handbooks issued by the government," he said. "So when David brought me to this group, it was just a whole new experience for me. I had been hanging around with kind of a rough crowd in the army and these people were just so friendly and loving. It was a small group of Christians that met every Thursday night for a little Bible study of their own. This group literally taught me to read by tutoring me in the Bible. As a result of that, after a period of about two or three months, I was able to read the book of Mark and it just revolutionized my life. To think that those little marks on that paper could have such a profound meaning was just amazing to me. Suddenly, I just wanted to read everything I could get my hands on. I joke about it now, but right after that experience, I went out and bought Edward Gibbon's *History of the Decline and Fall of the Roman Empire*. I was going to go out and read those whole three volumes. Of course, I never got past the first two chapters but that whole new level of wanting to read and discovering a whole new world was just so exciting."

Fleming said that the key to his success is not just keeping kids tuned in to his history classes. They also have to be aware of life's big picture.

"I want young people to understand that there is more to life than just the physical," Fleming said. "There is a body, mind and soul and all three of them must be fed."

Another key to Fleming's success is his upbringing. While many people would see his upbringing as a disadvantage,

Fleming took his own experiences from the rough, inner city area of Detroit and brought them into his own classroom with him. Now, some 40 years later, he's sharing his story with kids who are going through similar problems at home.

"I was born during the Depression and when my mom left me with my grandparents, it was with the assurance that, once she got a good job, she would send for me. She went to live in New York City and the good employment never came."

It would be more than 18 years before young Thomas would see his mother again. And, even then, it would just be for a short time.

"I didn't see my mother again until I left to go overseas," he said. "I was about 18 or 19 then. It was at that point that my mother told me that I didn't have a real dad and that I was the product of a Saturday night dance. Of course, I tried to make her think that it didn't bother me. But as soon as I was totally out of sight and headed back to the ship, I couldn't keep it in any longer and the tears started to flow like Niagara Falls. I was so sad when I found out that I didn't have a real daddy."

Fortunately, Fleming had grandparents who were there to help him while he was growing up. Gordon and Carrie Stark gave him a stable home life and, while Fleming will be the first to tell you that he didn't have the easiest of situations at home, it was stable enough that he didn't stray too far off course.

"Gordon and Carrie more than made up for the situation I had with my mother," he said. "They are Mom and Dad to me and I'm thankful for the influence that they had in my life."

After spending almost two years in Germany, Fleming was suddenly out of the army and looking for a job back in Detroit.

"I was back home, hanging out with my home boys in Detroit," he said. "They were doing crime, but I didn't know it. They got picked up by the police one day while I was out looking for a job. The police had gone over to my mom's house and told her to tell me that when I got home to just go on down to the police station and talk to the police. I didn't really think a lot about it but when I got down there they locked me up! I was just there one night, but that was enough."

Supposedly his friends had broken into a theater and the police had thought that Fleming had been involved in the caper.

"They said that my buddies had broken into a theater and they may have," Fleming said. "But after they let me out of jail the next day, I didn't wait around to find out what happened. I was so traumatized by that experience that I went straight down to the army recruiter's office and re-enlisted for another three years."

Back in the army, Fleming was back at the motor pool. During this stint, he learned new skills.

"When I went back in the army the second time, I learned to drive a jeep and a weapons carrier," he said. "When I got out of the army the first time, this was the only skill that I had. So, when I went back the second time, I graduated from the weapons carrier to a troop truck that would carry a whole platoon of 25 men. When I was shipped out the second time to France, I learned to drive both a tractor and a trailer and a five-ton dump truck because we were building a new air strip in France where I was stationed."

Three years later, however, Fleming found himself in the same situation as he did before he had re-enlisted.

"When I got out of the army, I had planned to get a job driving a truck," he said. "But the companies where I applied told me that my military training wasn't comparable to civilian training and that I had to go back to school and get an education. I wanted to drive commercial trucks because that's where the money was and I enjoyed doing it. But after they told me no, I had to think of another way to make a living."

So Fleming got a job on the assembly line at Chrysler.

"It only took me a few weeks to realize that I couldn't do that for the rest of my life," he said. "You see old men and young men there and I knew that I didn't want to make that my life's work. Every day, all day, that was your job.

"My job was to work on the motor heads. The motor has two heads on it and, when the head came by me, I had to flip it over and put two bolts in it with this kind of oily substance and then I had to flip it over and push it to the next guy. He would then put about 10 or 15 of these motors on a big wheel and then they would be wheeled over to another area where they would be sandblasted and cleaned up again. But you could see that, on that type of assembly line, I couldn't feed them to the next guy fast enough and he was always complaining to the foreman. Sometimes you were using an air hammer from overhead to put the bolts in. And, sometimes, if you did it too much, you would screw it too far down and it would actually go into the motor and ruin it. Then the motor becomes a dud. I was trying to make sure I didn't go down too far and so, as a result, I wasn't getting them to the next guy fast enough to suit him."

Interestingly enough, the problem worked itself out because, at that time, Chrysler was hiring some people for only 90 days.

"They would hire a lot of people for only 90 days so that you couldn't get your union status," Fleming said. "During my 90 days, I had decided that I was going to go to school. I recognized that I needed to learn to read better and that, if I was going to get anywhere in life, I needed to get an education."

Fleming began taking classes at the Detroit Bible Institute in 1957. But he'll be the first to tell you that he wasn't an instant success.

"Look at this," he said, as he dug through his briefcase and produced some of his old college transcripts. "Here's my whole grade sheet from Bible school. You can see right here where I flunked several classes in night school. And I show this to kids! I did make a few *A*'s as well, but that's only because the school was filled with the love of Christ."

He's laughing now as he looks back on those old college days.

Just as suddenly, however, he becomes serious. He's got his classroom face on again.

"Kids need to know that I didn't start out teaching school," he said. "They need to know that it wasn't easy for me and that education, true education, is not easy for anybody. It's something you have to work for. It's something you have to want."

From the Detroit Bible Institute, Fleming transferred to day school.

"At that point, I still didn't have my high school diploma," he said. "I realized that I had to do something about getting my G.E.D. or something because, as it was, the institute couldn't graduate me."

Fleming not only earned his G.E.D., he also received a bachelor's degree in religious education from William Tyndale College. He then went on to Eastern Michigan University, where he received a master's degree in special education.

"I tell kids that they have to capture the moment," he said. "And teachers have to be aware of teachable moments. A teachable moment is not just when something goes through the eyes and ears but when something goes through the eyes, ears and heart. It totally penetrates and that kind of teachable moment will stand out in their lives as they grow up and the other connectives will happen that will help them to start dealing with significant issues that tell them who they are."

Fleming added that a lot of the problems that youth have to deal with today are caused by what he calls "social mirrors."

"You cannot become independent as long as you are mentally dependent," he said. "We have so many people today that are living with social mirrors. Social mirrors are secondary greatness. If someone else tells me I'm cool, then I'm cool. If somebody else tells me this or that, I'm this or that. Instead of thinking like this, young people need to think about themselves in terms of primary greatness, which says, 'Hey, I'm all right! I'm powerfully and wonderfully made. I can do a lot of things!'"

It is at that point that the phone rings and the visitor excuses himself. Fleming's phone messages are getting through again and, apparently, so are his.

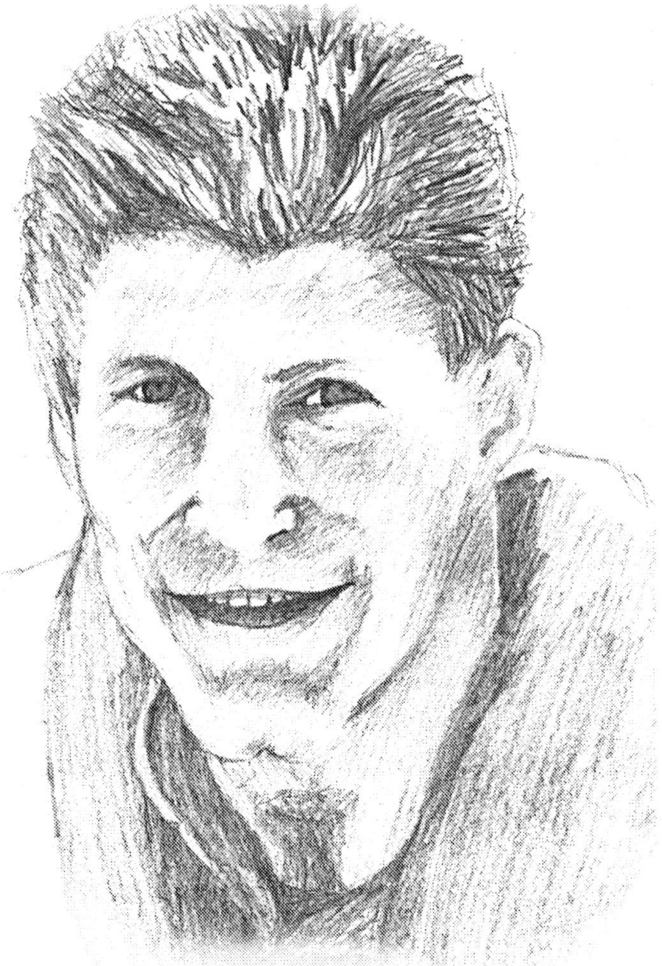

Chad Hennings

A Lesson In Commitment

Even if he never played a down in the National Football League, Chad Hennings would still be an impressive individual. In 1995, we interviewed Chad for the story that appears below, which originally ran in a special Super Bowl issue of Sports Spectrum Magazine. *Hennings, a U.S. Air Force Academy graduate and former combat pilot during the first Gulf War, talked about the rewards of staying faithful to Christ, his country and his family.*

Commitment. It's a word that's used a lot these days but so few of us really understand what it means. We change jobs, we change schools, we change our majors in college. If we are not happy, if we are not immediately successful in every endeavor we try, then there is a tendency to want to forget about that particular goal that we've set for ourselves and go try something else.

"There are too many people out there who want to take the easy way out," said Chad Hennings, the 6-foot-6 defensive tackle for the Dallas Cowboys. "What a lot people don't understand is that, to get anywhere in life, you have to work hard. There is no easy way to the top and you have to pay your dues."

A good part of Hennings' work ethic comes from his parents. Growing up on a 900-acre farm in Iowa, Hennings and his family are no strangers to hard work.

"My parents always told me to never quit anything," he said. "They told me that if was going to commit to something, commit to it to the very end. See it through. And, basically, that's what I have tried to do with anything that I've ever been involved in."

After high school, Hennings was accepted into the United States Air Force Academy in Colorado Springs, Colorado. It was a dream that he had pursued since he was a teenager and he was determined to be successful in both the rigors of military life and academics.

"I first became interested in going to the Air Force Academy when I was a sophomore in high school," he said. "At that time, military movies like *Top Gun* and *The Lords of Discipline* were out and that really started me thinking about going to the Air Force Academy. I've always been intrigued with the lifestyle of testing myself in a conflict situation. Pushing myself to the limits, sort of like a 'Rambo,' to see if I had what it takes to perform well in a pressure situation. That's the thing I enjoyed most about the Air Force Academy. We worked extremely hard but it was also extremely rewarding when you made it through."

Hennings was so dedicated to the Air Force that, unlike a lot of people in the military, he had a hard time leaving after four years.

"The thing I had a problem with was actually leaving the Air Force to go play football because I did make a commitment to the United States Air Force for eight years, not four," he said. "As it turned out, I was up to be released from my military obligation after four years because they were letting people do the early outs and, suddenly, I had a big decision to make. Naturally, I wanted to play pro football but I really didn't want to leave the Air Force because I felt like, in a sense, that I was quitting because, technically, I had committed for eight years and I wanted to honor that commitment."

But after a great deal of prayer and some long discussions with some of the other pilots, Hennings decided that he had fulfilled his obligation to his country and that it was okay to leave the military if he wanted to.

"I kept thinking about the words of Winston Churchill," he said, deepening his voice and doing his best Winston Churchill imitation. "Never, Never, Never, Never, Never give up!"

Hennings laughs at this point but suddenly gets serious again.

"It was difficult while I was in the Air Force not to be thinking about playing pro football because that's what I really wanted to do," he said. "But, for me, that really wasn't an option. I was committed to being in the United States Air Force and, while I often thought about playing football, I knew I had to suppress those thoughts and feelings because, at that time, that really wasn't an option."

When it suddenly became an option, however, Hennings was ready. And, to advance to that next level of play, Hennings knew he had to return to the same work habits that had made him successful in both high school and college.

"I look back on some of the things that I did on our farm in Iowa and I wonder how I did it," he said. "There were days where I would be out all afternoon in 95 degree temperatures bailing hay and straw and then, in the evenings, go work out on weights and then go run four miles. I was always dedicated to going out and working hard so that I could be the best."

Hennings added that, as he looks at the headlines today, not everybody agrees with him.

"From reading the headlines in the paper, you'll see that there are a lot of people who want to place the blame on everybody but themselves," he said. "Either racially or economically or whatever. There is only one way to become successful and that is to work hard. There is no easy way out."

At the U.S. Air Force Academy, Hennings learned the value of prioritizing things in his life. It is a skill that has served him well in the NFL.

"I took a class there that taught us that we had to rank things in one of three different categories - A, B, or C," Hennings said. "Category A was for things that had to be done today. Category B was for things that didn't have to be done for a day or so and Category C was for things that could be put off for another week. It's all just a matter of giving up unimportant things - give and take. One of the reasons that I think that students are all stressed in high school and college today is that they try to do too many things. They're just strung out with all these different activities that they have going on. So, instead of being successful at one thing, they wind up dropping out of everything because they are so frustrated. To put it in military terms, you have to 'pick your battles' and prioritize the things in your life that are the most important."

In 1992, after a four-year hiatus from football because of his military obligation, Hennings returned to the game. While he was one of the more highly touted rookies on the Cowboys at training camp that summer, it would still be another year or so before the former Outland Trophy

Award-winner would make the kind of impact that he did for the Falcons at the United States Air Force Academy.

"My first year was a difficult one because I just wanted to play," he said. "I just wanted an opportunity to get out there and show what I could do but that wasn't happening."

Hennings was de-activated for the first five games of the 1992 season and was in uniform for the next game against Kansas City but didn't play. For the next two games, while the Cowboys were in Los Angeles and then hosted the Eagles, Hennings found himself back on the de-activated list.

Not one to sit around and wait for things to happen, Hennings went to then-coach Jimmy Johnson and asked if he could play on special teams. Johnson agreed and Hennings proved to be the "wedge-buster" on special teams in a 37-3 route of the Lions. He supplied a couple of key hits on the way to tying for the team lead in special teams tackles that day. Because of his success on special teams, Johnson also used him at defensive tackle in games against the Cardinals, Giants and Eagles. Then, when the post-season arrived and the Cowboys were gearing up for their first Super Bowl appearance in years, Hennings made his presence felt, getting three tackles in post-season play as his stock in the Cowboy organization grew.

"Chad is one of the most dedicated and focused individuals that I've ever had the privilege to work with," said former Dallas Defensive Coordinator Butch Davis. "He has great maturity and self-confidence. I've never seen a harder worker or a more disciplined player. Some of that character, of course, comes from the fact that he grew up on a farm and from his military experience as a fighter pilot. But, in my opinion, Chad's great character comes from his deep faith in, and his devotion to, Jesus Christ."

It was that commitment to Christ that helped Hennings learn patience during his first two years with the Cowboys.

"The early part of 1992 was a little frustrating for me because I wasn't getting to play," he said. "So I volunteered for kickoffs. Here I was, this big defensive lineman running down on kickoffs. I've always felt that you had to make your own opportunities and then make the most of them and that's what I was trying to do in that game against the Lions."

Patience and hard work. For Hennings, they are the one-two punch in a formula for a successful career both on and off the field.

"One of the things that the Lord has taught me a lot about over the past two years is being patient and still maintaining a strong work ethic," Hennings said. "Every time I've worked hard, things have eventually gone my way. Maybe not initially, but certainly in the end. It's really not a matter of luck, it's a matter of making your own opportunities. And, when those opportunities come up, you've got to make the most of them."

While football is an important part of Henning's life now, he still makes Jesus the number one priority in his life.

"Growing as a Christian is definitely Priority A," he said. "It's something that my wife Tammy and I work on every day. We'll usually go to bed 30 to 45 minutes early and read our Bible together and talk about the verses that we just read and then pray together. It's just amazing how God has blessed us."

While growing up on his parent's farm in Iowa, Chad was a devout Lutheran. He was in church most Sundays and could often be found studying the Word of God.

But it was while he was stationed in England that Chad came into a personal relationship with Christ.

"Since I grew up Lutheran and went to church almost every Sunday, I really thought I was a Christian," he said. "I studied the Bible, I prayed, I did all the things that I thought would get me to heaven. But, when I was in the Air Force and stationed in England, I got to know a chaplain from the Air Force and he sort of rekindled the fire. I think it was at that point that I truly accepted Christ as my Savior and dedicated my life to Him. At that point we started going out and having Bible studies and just actively pursued how to grow in our faith. From that day on, my relationship with the Lord has grown five-fold and I'm so thankful that He's given me the blessings that He has."

This new relationship with the Lord has also had a domino effect on Chad's family.

"It's really exciting to see how my family has grown spiritually," he said. "My brothers and sisters have really started to blossom in their faith over the last few years so it's really been a growing process for all of us."

Oddly enough, Hennings said it was some initial philosophical and religious differences that ultimately drew the family a lot closer.

"I think that we started to grow before that, but those differences have really brought us together because what we started to do was to really research the different issues and find out what it means to truly be a Christian and how one can truly be saved and not get into some of this 'New Age' theology that seems to be so prevalent in our culture today," he said. "It's really been exciting to follow Christ and see the things he's doing in my life and the lives of my family."

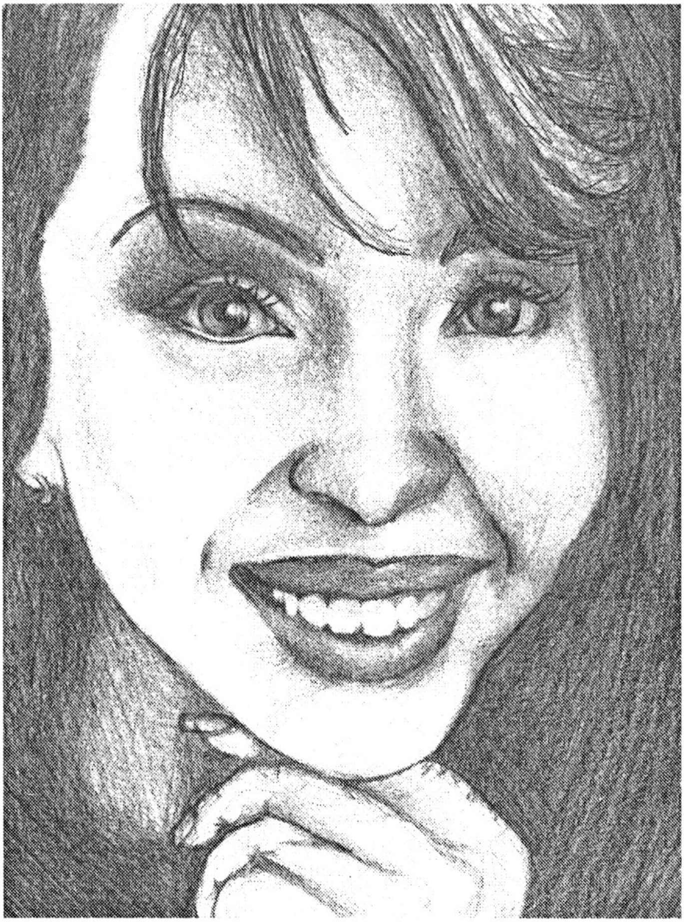

Gladys Knight

Just Gladys

When you hear some of Gladys Knight's music from the 1960s and 1970s, it sounds just as good today as it did then. When we went back and listened to the recording from our June, 1994 interview with her, we both shook our heads in amazement. Did we really just ask Gladys Knight to sing a few bars of Midnight Train to Georgia? *For all her talent and success, she still remains one of the most humble people in the entertainment industry today. The story that appears below was written shortly after we spoke with her in the summer of 1994.*

She was in San Diego between sessions of a video shoot and, as always, Gladys Knight was on the go.

"I've just been rippin' and runnin', trying to find these little minutes," she said, laughing. "You'd think that things would slow down sometime, but they just don't seem to."

Nor are they likely to when one is blessed with the talent of Gladys Knight.

Her musical career began at the age of four, when she started singing at her local church.

"I had no idea that I wanted to be a singer or anything else at that age," she said. "It was all the production of my mom and dad saying that we have a child here that has some talent and we need to try to promote that."

By the age of seven, Knight was auditioning for "The Ted Mack Amateur Hour" and coming away with the show's $2,000 grand prize.

A few years later, at the encouragement of her mother, she formed a group with her brother, Merald (Bubba), sister Brenda and cousins William and Elenor. They adopted another cousin's nickname, James "Pip" Woods and became the Pips. When the question of turning professional came up, Brenda and Elenor opted to go to college rather than risk the uncertain world of entertainment, while Edward Patton joined the group.

As Gladys became a teenager, she found that there were other things that she enjoyed.

"As a teenager I lived a very normal life," she said. "I went to public schools. I had friends. And I lived a very normal life. I wanted to go to basketball practice and I was on the track team and when my parents told me that I couldn't go to basketball practice or to a track meet because we were going to New York for a performance, I was upset because I wanted to go to my track meet. So I went through those things."

In 1965, Knight signed with Motown Records and her career took off. She and the Pips, along with groups like Diana Ross and the Supremes, Smokey Robinson and the Miracles, and The Four Tops helped build a strong foundation for the newly formed Motown Records.

"It was an incredibly exciting time for all of us," Knight said. "At that time, you had a lot of things opening up and it wasn't just the music when you really stop to think about it. The 1960s were a time for progress and rebirth and desegregation. The same thing happened in music. We had the chance to be exposed to other races of people, we got a chance to play places that we had not played before like the Copa Cabañas and be on the Ed Sullivan Show and all these other kinds of things. It was just a very exciting time."

By the mid-1970s, Gladys Knight and the Pips were firmly entrenched in Billboard Magazine's Top Ten with a string of hits that included *Midnight Train to Georgia, Best Thing that Ever Happened to Me, I Heard It Through The Grapevine* and *If I Were Your Woman.*

She and the Pips traveled all over the world, won numerous Grammy Awards and had several gold records. The group became synonymous with style and grace as the gentle Motown sounds of Gladys and her cousins the Pips were heard everywhere around the world.

One of the group's biggest hits came in 1973 when they topped the charts with *Midnight Train to Georgia.* In a summer filled with news about Watergate and rising gasoline prices, Knight's smooth style and rich voice seemed to remind listeners all over the country that things were not as bad as they seemed.

"I didn't help write *Midnight Train to Georgia,* but I did help produce it," Knight said. "It was really no different than any other song that I would choose. I always look for lyrical content and how the story line progressed and whether it had merit that would touch people's lives. I also looked for how relevant the story was. That's what I would look for personally. Then I would look for the melody. Did it sing well? Was it something that I felt comfortable with in the way it was put together? Then I would look for the melody. Did it sing well for me personally? Did it make me move? And that's how I chose all my songs. It just turned out that *Midnight Train* was a song that touched a lot of people. Plus, there are a lot of things that go together in this business that make a song happen. We happened to be in a space at that time, with the right company with the right people who really believed in us. We were also at the top of what we were doing and the song got the exposure that it deserved. Otherwise, *Midnight Train* would have never been the song that it was."

By the late 1980s, the group had won every award imaginable. Gold Records. Platinum Records. American Music Awards. Top 10 hit after Top 10 hit.

"It kind of reached a point where we asked ourselves, 'What else can we do?'" Knight said. "We had won every major award imaginable and had performed all over the world. I think we were all getting just a little bit complacent. I think that was the whole reason we decided to split up."

By the early 1990s, Gladys Knight and the Pips had slowly become Gladys Knight. Period. Sans Pips.

Knight will be the first to tell you that her fans didn't exactly take the news well at first. For many, Gladys Knight without the Pips was the equivalent to the Beatles breaking up. No one was exactly sure what a "Pip" was, mind you, but they knew that this was not right. How could Gladys do this, anyway? What would happen to the Pips? Where would they go? What would they do? *Gladys, Say it Ain't So!*

"What people don't realize is that I'm solo now," she said. "But there are a lot of people who think that I was born and raised with the Pips. Yes, I spent 30-something years of my life with the Pips but I had a solo career long before there was a Pip and a lot of people have a hard time fathoming that.

Those guys are family and always will be. But it just got to the point that we all needed to go on and do other things."

She paused.

"It was about growing," she continued. "We have done this a number of times before, but you have to be so careful about image and all of the things that go with that when you are a performer. Whenever I would do something solo under the banner of Gladys Knight and the Pips, we were still together. People, because they didn't want anything to happen to that entity, wouldn't support what I would do. They would look at it like I was trying to be a big shot. But we always looked at it like any of us could do anything that we wanted to do under the umbrella of this group."

Still, Knight said she was beginning to feel restricted.

"There were things that I wanted to do that couldn't be done in the structure of the group," she said. "As long as the group was active, it was like that was our whole energy and I think that's why we were as successful as we were. I mean, we ate, slept and dreamed Gladys Knight and the Pips and that didn't leave a lot of space for anything else. Even though we had the freedom to do other things as individuals, it seemed that we never got a chance to do any of those things because of each of our commitments to the group. I really wanted to go on and do other things. I wanted to write. I wanted to act and I wanted to produce and whenever you get into things like that, that takes time as well. And commitment. So, if there was something that Gladys Knight and the Pips wanted to do, well, you had to make a decision. So we just decided that, hey, let's just grow as individuals now and that's how we got to that point."

These days, Knight is staying busy with her video projects, concert tours and record promotions. She's quick to tell you that show business can take its toll on a family.

The endless concert tours, rehearsals and recording sessions make marriage and family life difficult if not impossible.

Knight is no stranger to heartache. Her first two marriages ended in divorce.

"It is probably one of the most painful and hurtful things a person can go through because the hurt is so great and the disappointment is so great," she said. "But I think that if both parties would focus more on their relationship with Christ and try to realize that, hey, we're both human beings here and that we aren't perfect, more marriages could be saved. Divorces get so nasty, so hateful, because of the hurt involved. You always hear about those self-help programs that tell you things like 'You can do it' and how you can be successful at something. But you never seem to hear about how to get through a time when things don't go well and you're not successful. You don't hear about how to have grace in things when you don't make it and we all need to hear that.

"In my case, it was my faith that kept me going through those difficult times. You know that there is someone greater who cares about what happens to you."

Like most of those who are successful in life, Knight said she has had a great supporting cast.

"Finding a sense of balance is something that everybody has to be aware of and something that everybody has to contribute to," she said. "My children have made tremendous sacrifices for me to be able to do what I do. And I just love them and thank them for being the kind of children that they are, even though I wasn't there for them while they were growing up. They were born into this.

"There were a lot of times when I wasn't there when they had the measles or I would miss some important part of their lives or programs but they were always understanding. I didn't overcompensate for not being there when I was home.

It was just a part of our lives and this was what God intended for me to do and I just tried to do the best that I could. But I gave to my children whenever I had the opportunity to and I kept them with me whenever I had the chance to keep them with me.

"I think quality time is important. A lot of people say that and it has gotten to be a cliché, but I really meant it. My children have made tremendous sacrifices for me and I made tremendous sacrifices for them. It was 14 years between my first marriage and my second marriage because I devoted myself to my work and my children."

With that, Gladys Knight politely excused herself. She was "Rippin' and Runnin'" again, off to finish her video shoot, where she would sing some of her latest hits.

Like a rare jewel, Knight is a musician who seems to be improving with age.

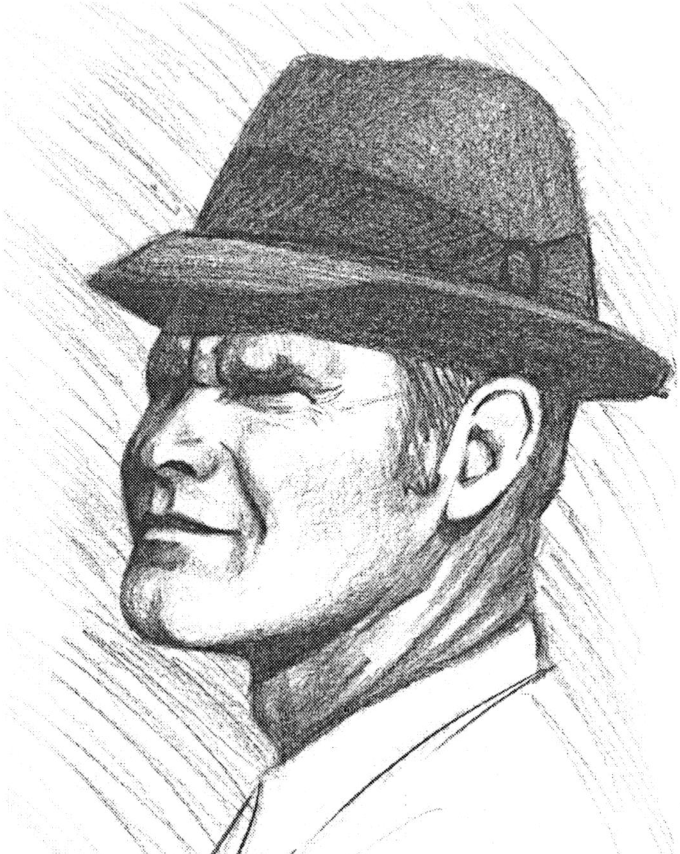

Tom Landry

Amazing Grace

The world lost a good friend in February of 2000 when Tom Landry succumbed to cancer. The intriguing thing about Landry was that the more people knew about him, the more they respected him. When reporters dug deep into the life of Tom Landry, they didn't find dirt. They found buried treasure. Most people never knew he was involved in a prison ministry until shortly before he died. Many people never knew that he was an extremely skilled airplane pilot. Most everyone knew, however, that he was a man of amazing grace. In this 1994 interview, Landry talked about how he was able to keep his cool during one of the most difficult times of his life.

February 25, 1989. For Cowboy fans, it was the end of an era.

It was on this day that Tom Landry, the only head coach that the Dallas Cowboys ever had, suddenly became the only head coach ever to be fired by the Cowboys.

Jerry Jones, an enthusiastic newcomer to the NFL, had bought the team from Bum Bright and had now planned to bring his old college roommate and Miami Hurricane Head Coach Jimmy Johnson in to replace Landry.

Before all of this became official, however, Jones had flown Johnson to Dallas, where the two former Razorbacks dined at one of Landry's favorite restaurants, Mia's Mexican Restaurant. A picture of Jones and Johnson appeared in the *Dallas Morning News* the next day, Saturday, February 25. Landry not only recognized the restaurant but also the table where the two sat.

Still, with all the speculation, Landry had heard nothing official. Neither he nor Cowboys President and General Manager Tex Schramm had heard directly from either Jones or Cowboys owner Bum Bright as to what was happening with the sale of the team.

Various reports had indicated that investors were scared off by Bright's asking price for the team. Other, unconfirmed reports indicated that a local group was trying to get the necessary funds together to buy the team out from under Jones. Denver oilman Marvin Davis' name also surfaced as a possible buyer for the team.

So, with all the speculation and nothing still official, Landry decided to fly his small, private plane to his home in Austin and enjoy a round of golf. After completing the first hole, however, he got a call from Schramm. Schramm and Jones were coming down to see him and the news wasn't good.

There was nothing to do but wait so Landry, his son Tom Jr. and his son-in-law, Gary Childers, played out the rest of the round.

"I don't remember much about the round," Landry recalled in his autobiography, *Tom Landry*. "I do recall it was tougher than usual to concentrate on the weak points of my game."

Jones and Schramm arrived and met Landry in one of the clubhouses. Jones had told him the news that Landry and the rest of the football world had heard for the past three days but didn't want to believe.

Jones had bought the team and was bringing Jimmy Johnson in to coach it.

"I don't remember much of anything he said after that," Landry would later write. "A jumble of feelings crowded my mind. Anger. Sadness. Frustration. Disappointment. Resignation.

"Jones said something about wishing that there was some way he could make this easier for me. And I guess that's the only time I let my frustration and anger about the uncertainty and secretive events of the past week come through, because I told him I didn't think the situation had been handled the way it should have been.

"He apologetically tried to explain why things had developed the way they had over the preceding few days. But we all knew there wasn't much to say at this point."

Landry, to his credit, had little to say to the media or anyone else about the situation. He refused to blast Jones publicly even at a time when every major media outlet in the Dallas-Fort Worth area was highly critical of Jones and his handling of the whole situation. Even columnists and commentators who where were calling for Landry's job after his last season, 1988, in which the team finished 3-13, were saying that Landry should have been allowed to coach one more season and then retire. Jones, they said, at least owed him that much.

But if you heard anything negative about Jones, it didn't come from Landry. In fact, he took the news much like he did when tight end Jackie Smith dropped that touchdown pass from Roger Staubach in Super Bowl XIII against the Pittsburgh Steelers. Stoically. Expressionless. Without emotion, even though inside he might have been dying a thousand deaths.

Now, five years later, Landry looks back on that day with some of the same graciousness and class that he showed at the Hidden Hills Country Club in Austin on the day he was fired.

"When Jerry Jones had the opportunity to buy the club, I'm sure that he was just real excited and wasn't really thinking about what was taking place within Tex Schramm, myself and all of the other Cowboys who didn't even know what was being done at the time," Landry said.

"You know, it really kind of made it easy for me because when he said I was out, I had already heard it on television. I felt bad for my assistants, of course, and a number of our players and a number of our organizational people, Tex Schramm in particular, because they were all a part of our team and weren't being treated real well. But for me, personally, I think God just closed that door and opened a new one.

"The thing that helped me most was the parade they had for me a few months later in April. It was different from most parades because what I sensed as I rode in the car downtown was that the people were really feeling for me personally, not that they had lost me as a head coach. It was more than that for them. They felt sorry for me and they showed it. And this really helped. When people care about you like that, you know that there is something better.

"It's incredible to think about how many people, all over the country, no matter where I go, will come up and tell me things like 'I grew up with you and the Dallas Cowboys.' And it makes you feel good to know that you had an impact on people's lives."

In Tom Landry's autobiography, he called it "Firing Day" but, when you really talk to him about it, a better title for this chapter might be entitled "A Day for New Beginnings."

Yes, Landry's coaching days may have come to an end but his days as a speaker and his work with groups like the Fellowship of Christian Athletes and other Christian organizations were just beginning.

"I'm busier now than I ever was coaching football," Landry said. "With football, life was pretty predictable as far as where you would be at a certain time of the year. Now, when you are in the business and speaking world, new things come up from time to time and life stays pretty interesting. I really travel a tremendous amount right now, not only speaking but attending board meetings and things that I am on. It has kept me very busy."

Without the rigors of football, Landry has found more time to spend with his family and to speak to young people.

"I think athletes and coaches can have a tremendous impact on young people, if they want to take the time to do it," he said. "It is really a shame when you see an athlete shy away from a youngster and not give them an autograph. Regardless of how busy I am or how much I have to do, I usually try to take the time to sign an autograph because I think that is a part of our responsibility. I think you miss a great deal if your life is so calloused that you can not stop and be a role model for these youngsters coming up because we need it more today in the United States than we ever have."

Landry added that, as a coach, it was difficult to share the Gospel of Christ with his players, simply because he had to maintain a certain distance from them in order not to weaken them.

"What we basically tried to do when I was coaching was to create an atmosphere where the team chaplain would take a large role in that," Landry said. "As head coach, you don't want to weaken a player by your relationship with him. I've always felt that you have to have a distance from your players as head coach. If you do, then you will challenge them to be all they can be. I think that is just so important.

"When I was the defensive coach for the Giants, I played cornerback and also coached the defense. In the 1950s when I played, you only had four coaches. It was the greatest time that I've ever had coaching because, really, I could relate to these players, I could be their buddy. I could be a coach and everything else, too. But that is so different than being a head coach. As head coach, everything is in your power to make the thing go and, if you treat it that way, then you should have a successful team."

And Landry is no stranger to successful teams. After an 0-11-1 start during the Cowboys' expansion season of 1960, Landry quickly moved the club into an era of respectability. By 1965 the club had reached the .500 mark with a 7-7 record. The next year they won the Eastern Division but lost to the Green Bay Packers in the championship game.

Playoff appearances in 1967, 1968 and 1969 seasoned the club and, by 1970, they were in the Super Bowl against the Baltimore Colts.

Colt fans will never forget Baltimore kicker Jim O'Brien's game-winning field goal in the final seconds that won the game. For Dallas, Bob Lilly's 50-yard helmet toss after that kick seemed to sum up the season and the Cowboys' frustration.

Close but no cigar. Cliché? Certainly. But it was a phrase that seemed to sum up those five difficult Cowboy seasons.

Dallas, in spite of the tremendous success they had in just reaching the playoffs, was becoming known as "The team that couldn't win the big one."

Landry quickly began to study ways to get the team over the hump. He brought in an industrial psychologist who took confidential surveys and did psychological evaluations of the team. He worked harder at studying game films to analyze opponents' weaknesses. He designed new offensive and defensive strategies.

But, perhaps more importantly, he put two new key cogs in the Cowboy wheel. A running back from Yale by the name of Calvin Hill came in and ran wild over opposing defenses. Another player, this one a quarterback who was drafted out the U.S. Naval Academy, proved to be enough to turn the tide against Green Bay and the Cleveland Browns.

Navy mid-shipman Roger Staubach was just the tonic the Cowboys needed. Self-confident, a natural leader and a strong Christian, Staubach lead the Cowboys to victory in Super Bowl VI in 1972 against the upstart Miami Dolphins.

"That was probably my greatest thrill in football," Landry said. "For years, we had tried to get over the top but just couldn't seem to win the big game. That game against Miami took the pressure off and gave us the confidence we needed to win the big games."

Landry added that, in today's game, because of cable television and increased revenue that can be generated through NFL licensing and other areas, a head coach's job is much tougher now than it ever has been.

"When I first started with the Cowboys, we had a great, great owner in Clint Murchison," Landry said. "He gave me a 10-year contract when I hadn't won but 10 games and was a natural leader from that standpoint in that he showed a great deal of confidence in me at a time when he really didn't have to.

"But owners are different now and, to a certain extent, they have to be. They have so much invested in their teams and so much at stake that they can't help but be.

"The cap on salaries is just part of what happens. Now, we are at a time in professional football where the owners are getting involved in the personnel decisions that are so important to a head coach. Pretty soon, the head coach starts looking over his shoulder because he knows, really, that he is going to have a tough time keeping his job when it comes right down to it."

Landry added that, once owners do get involved in day-to-day decisions of a team, small situations turn into big deals.

"In the practices, in the locker rooms and on the sidelines, so many things happen that aren't meant for those outside that context to see," Landry observed. "When someone from the outside sees those things go on, they think it's a major problem because they really don't know the context of the situation. In recent years, it seems it has become more and more difficult for head coaches to handle these problems within the confines of the team."

Another problem for head coaches, Landry added, is the increased pressure to take a team to the Super Bowl.

"The major goal in professional football now is to reach the Super Bowl," Landry said. "It's not enough to go to the playoffs or have a winning season anymore. Everybody's goal is to go to the Super Bowl and very few teams have the opportunity to do that. Unless you win the Super Bowl, you feel like you haven't been successful. That's why our Super Bowl win against Miami felt so good."

Landry's two Super Bowl rings and five Super Bowl appearances will always rank him high among past and present NFL coaches. But the grace he showed on that sunny, winter day in Austin, Texas when he was unceremoniously released by Jerry Jones will always rank him high in the hearts and minds of football fans everywhere.

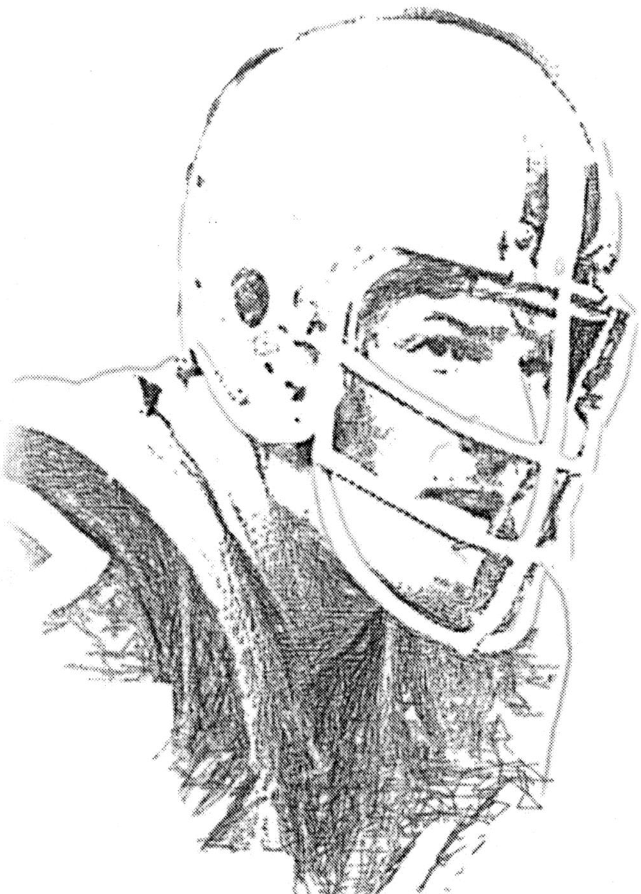

Bob Lilly

The Dangers of Alcohol

Cowboy fans will always remember Bob Lilly throwing his helmet about 50 yards after Jim O'Brien's last-second field goal in Super Bowl V helped the Baltimore Colts defeat the Cowboys and become world champs. The next year, however, Lilly left another indelible image. In Super Bowl VI, he chased Miami's Bob Griese down and sacked him for a 29-yard loss as Dallas finally shed its tag as "Bridesmaids" and won the Super Bowl. But, after years of waiting for a Super Bowl ring, what happens when your dreams finally come true? In 1991, we talked with Lilly about life after football as well as some of his thoughts after the Cowboys won Super Bowl VI.

It has been more than 10 years since former Dallas Cowboy Bob Lilly came across an accident on a Texas highway that would change his life forever.

Several months before that accident, he had just been awarded professional football's most prestigious honor when he was named to the Pro Football Hall of Fame in

Canton, Ohio. At the same time, Lilly owned a Coors Beer distributorship in Waco and, after another late night at the office, he was driving home when he saw an overturned truck on the highway.

"I don't remember exactly what year it was, but it was right after I was elected to the hall of fame in late 1980 or early 1981," Lilly said during a recent telephone interview from his home in Graham, Texas. "I was driving down the highway late at night and I saw a pickup overturned and stopped to see if I could help. There were two boys in the truck and they looked like they were about 16 or 17 years old. When I opened one of the doors of the truck, I saw several cans of my beer roll out. There were also some other brands in there and it really doesn't make any difference what they were. The main thing is that, at that point, I felt a conviction to get out of the beer business. I mean, here I was a quote, unquote 'celebrity' and I was selling beer. Seeing those kids in that pickup made me realize that, at least for me, being in the beer business is not the kind of business that God wanted me in."

While that incident proved to be the turning point, Lilly said it was really just one of several things that eventually convinced him to get out of the beer business.

"There were a number of things that led to me getting out of it," he said. "First of all, both my wife Ann and I became born-again believers. We had gone to church all of our lives and I really do feel like I was a Christian while I was in high school but I just fell away from the Lord.

"In 1981, I rededicated my life to Him and that decision really started to change my perspective on some things. I never lost my communion with the Lord, but I could still feel myself falling away from Him. I was working so hard at my business that, really, my business came first, my family second and the Lord was third or fourth or wherever I could work him in."

Lilly added that his wife Ann was a major influence in his decision to rededicate his life to the Lord and live for Him.

"Ann had become a born-again Christian a few years after I had retired but I was working awfully hard at my new business. There is a lot of competition in the beer business and I was working hard because I was new at all this. I had retired from football in 1975 and was starting over. My peers in college were all established by the time I was out of football, but my career in business was just starting and I knew I had to work hard if I was going to be successful."

Those late nights and long hours spent at the business gradually began to take their toll on Lilly as he soon realized that he wanted to pursue other interests.

"At that particular time, I had other businesses and I really wanted to get away from those 12- and 14-hour days at the beer distributorship," he said. "I had kids at home and I wanted to spend more time with them before they were grown. It was really getting to the point where I was literally gone all the time. Even though I had been retired from football for a number of years, people were still calling me and wanting me to speak at various things. When you are in business, you almost feel that, if you don't do it, it is going to hurt your business so I always hated to turn someone down. I had really been stressed out at that time and all those things - the need to spend more time with my family, my re-dedication to the Lord and that accident - all those things combined made me realize that I wanted to sell my beer distributorship and go do something else."

Lilly added that another problem with the beer business was all the Catch-22s that he had to deal with.

"As a beer distributor, it's hard to just turn your advertising people loose on the public like that and tell them that they have to encourage as many people as they can to buy your product," Lilly said. "Beer companies are going to have to start spending more for education about alcohol and the dangers of it than they are in the actual advertising and I think we will start to see more of that in the future as beer companies begin to realize the dangers of alcohol."

Those dangers, however, are often ignored by the young people of this country, Lilly said.

"There is a lot of abuse of alcohol and I learned that when I was calling on nightclubs and bars while I owned my beer distributorship," Lilly said. "But that was mostly among adults. What I didn't see was the alcohol abuse among teenagers. There is a big problem with teenage alcohol abuse in this country. When I went off to college, we'd have a beer every once in a while, but we never abused it like a lot of teenagers seem to do today. I think alcohol is much more accepted in our culture than drugs are. And the reason for that is that our society really comes down on hard drugs but beer and other forms of alcohol are things that are tolerated."

Lilly added that society's views on alcohol have changed a great deal since he was a boy growing up in rural Texas.

"When I was growing up, alcoholism was a very serious thing and was looked down upon in the community," he said. "Alcoholics were shunned and it brought shame and disgrace not only for the alcoholic but also to his whole family. Now, I think hard drugs are in the news so much that beer is almost like water to people. You hear people every day who say things like 'Hey, it can't hurt you.' But that is wrong. It is a drug and it can hurt you if you abuse it."

Like a lot of society's ills these days, Lilly said that, in most cases, alcohol abuse among teenagers can be traced back to the breakdown of the family.

"Basically, I think it comes down to the breakdown of the home and the family unit," he said. "A lot of the parents in this country are divorced and I think it comes down to the fact that no one is keeping an eye on the kids."

With four children of their own, Bob and his wife Ann are no strangers to the problems and temptations that young people face on a daily basis. Their oldest three children - Bob Lilly Jr., Michelle and Chris are all grown now. Up until he graduated from high school a few years ago, their youngest son Mark faced all the pressures that any other high school student faces, Lilly said.

"We tried to educate Mark, and all our kids for that matter, about alcohol and the dangers of it," Lilly said. "We are fortunate in that we live in a pretty small community where most of the families know each other and we are able to keep an eye on who Mark runs around with. He's driving now and I've educated him on the penalties involved with drinking and driving and how he could lose his license. I also watch who he runs around with and my wife and I will have to cull out an unruly friend once in a while. But I think it's a parent's job to see to it that their kids hang around with the right type of people. It's tough for a mother whose working to do that these days and I think that's where a lot of the problem lies. Being aware of the problems that alcohol can cause start at home and, with so many homes split because of divorce, the kids of our country are not being educated properly about the dangers of alcohol."

Life After Super Bowl VI - *"Is This All There Is?"*

"We buckled down in 1972 and beat the Miami Dolphins in Super Bowl VI very decisively, 24-3," Lilly said. "But I'll never forget the morning after the game.

"Football had been eleven years of my life and I had accomplished all of my goals. I wasn't sophisticated in setting goals, but my first goal was to make All-America, my second goal was to make All-Pro and my third goal was to win a Super Bowl. Now, these things had been accomplished and even the goals of being affluent had come true. I had money, prestige and all the honors.

"About 6:30 a.m. on the morning after the Super Bowl, I walked out on the parking lot of our hotel in New Orleans. I was getting ready to leave for the Pro Bowl in Los Angeles. There were beer bottles, beer cans and all kinds of pop bottles, programs and pom-poms from the night before. I remember stumbling around and saying, 'Is this all there is?' This was 11 years of my life and I had accomplished all those goals and yet I was hollow inside. It was over; the elation and joy had burst like a balloon.

"I remembered something a man from West Texas told me one time. 'Every man has a God hole; you can try to fill it with anything you want and you just can't get satisfied until you fill it with Jesus. In fact, the more you try to fill it, the bigger the hole gets until you find Jesus."

Unfortunately, the hole in Lilly's soul just kept getting bigger.

"I still wasn't through," he said. "I played three more years, but my focus was on accumulating material things. My wife, Ann, and I lived in a very nice neighborhood in North Dallas and we had some real affluent neighbors who were always having parties and so I thought that this must be where it's at. But I still felt this emptiness inside."

A few years later, one of Lilly's neighbors invited Ann to go hear an evangelist speak.

"Ann went with her and decided to give her life to Jesus and become a Christian," Lilly said.

Ann started going out of her way to make Lilly feel special. Special meals, love notes on the refrigerator and other things convinced Lilly that Ann's life had changed.

"She seemed so happy all the time," Lilly said. "One day I came home and she was listening to the Bible on tape and another day I saw where she had the TV turned to a Christian TV station. I would act all tough and not concerned, but I would listen to the tapes of the Bible with her and soon I was getting this hunger inside me because I knew that she had something that I didn't have.

"Well, this continued for about two and a half years and I finally went to Ann and said, 'I don't know what you have got, but I want it.'

"As I mentioned earlier, I had accepted Christ as my Savior when I was in high school and really felt like I was a Christian at that time but I had fallen away from the Lord. In 1981, I re-dedicated my life to the Lord and, suddenly, the light came back into my life. Once I made Christ the Lord of my life, I began to feel a great hunger for the Word of God. I got some tapes and I listened to them whenever I was in the car. I went through the New Testament 14 times that year.

"What I like to tell people is that Jesus Christ can change your life in the same way He's changed mine," Lilly added. "Don't let the emptiness of material goods and popularity be a substitute for the genuine peace and happiness that come from knowing Jesus in a personal way. Give Him your life and experience the most rewarding and fulfilling life you can know."

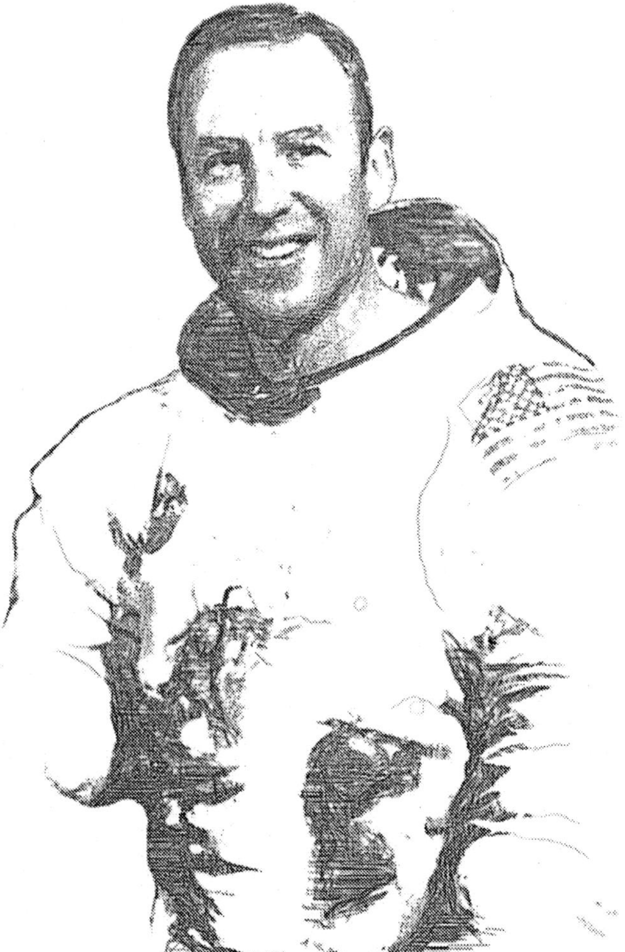

Jim Lovell

Bilirubin Blues

Some would call it "good fortune." Others would simply refer to it as "serendipity." But no matter what you call it, the authors were thankful to have the opportunity to interview former astronaut Jim Lovell in January of 1996 just before a fundraising dinner at a Dallas hotel. As Jim Lovell proves in this story, sometimes a little bit of stubbornness can lead to a great deal of success.

One of the most popular movies of 1995 was Ron Howard's "Apollo 13," starring Tom Hanks as Apollo 13 commander Jim Lovell.

The movie, based on Lovell's book *Lost Moon*, captured the imagination of the world and, in a sense, has made Lovell a hero all over again, some 25 years after his Apollo 13 heroics.

Apollo 13 never realized its mission of landing Lovell, Jack Swigert and Fred Haise on the moon. But the crew's courage and resourcefulness allowed them to get home safely.

In the world of space exploration, Lovell is one of the great American heroes. If you saw the way he conducted himself at Dallas Christian School's Vision 21 Banquet held at the Fairmont Hotel in Dallas Saturday, you could not help but be impressed.

There were slightly more than 900 guests in attendance at this banquet and Lovell probably signed about 2,000 autographs and posed for hundreds of pictures. He did it all with the same matter-of-fact diligence that he showed when he was orbiting the moon or, in his earlier years, working as a military test pilot.

Suddenly, the fickle footprint of fate has found the likable Lovell again, which is interesting when you think about the fact that he flunked his first physical examination during NASA's initial pilot testing program in January of 1958.

"I was in the very first group of 110 pilots that were tested for the space program," Lovell said during a press conference before the banquet. "They would give us physicals in groups of six or seven and they ran all kinds of tests on us."

According to Lovell's book, *Lost Moon* (which was re-titled *Apollo 13* to capitalize on the popularity of the movie) astronauts were submitted to grueling tests in order to qualify for the space program.

"Candidates for the space program," Lovell wrote in *Lost Moon,* "would have their livers injected with dye, their inner ears filled with cold water, their muscles punctured by electrified needles, their intestines filled with radioactive barium, their prostate glands squeezed, their sinuses probed and their stomachs pumped, their blood drawn, their scalps and chests plastered with electrodes and their bowels evacuated by diagnostic enemas at the rate of up to six per day."

After all that, Lovell said only one thing kept him from passing his physical.

"I had a high bilirubin count," he said, repeating a line in his book. "Bilirubin is a red pigment in your liver that could indicate the presence of hepatitis, malaria or yellow jaundice. I wasn't even sick at the time, but the doctors still wouldn't pass me."

Lost Moon gives a detailed discussion between Lovell and his doctor in 1958:

"Well you do, Lieutenant. We all do. It's a natural liver pigment, but you can have too much of it," the doctor said.

"Can it make me sick?" Lovell asked.

"Not really. It just means that you've been sick."

"And if I'm better now, there's no reason I can't go on with the program."

"Lieutenant, I have five men out there who don't have a bilirubin problem, and 26 more on the way who probably don't. I have to base my decision on something. I know you've been through a lot in the past week, and we thank you for your time."

"Couldn't we repeat the liver test?" Lovell ventured. "Maybe it was wrong."

"We already did," said the doctor.

"It wasn't. But we do thank you for your time."

"You know," Lovell persisted, "if you only accepted perfect specimens, sir, you'll only wind up with one kind of data. Taking someone with a little anomaly means you'll learn even more."

The doctor closed Lovell's file, pushed it aside, and looked up.

"We thank you," the doctor repeated slowly, "for your time."

The story, of course, could have ended right there. Fortunately for Lovell and the rest of the crew of Apollo 13, though, it didn't.

"I was dejected about getting rejected," Lovell recalled, smiling as he thought back to that day in January of 1958. "At that time, all those test results were confidential. I had a neighbor who was a doctor and I took him into my confidence and explained the situation to him. He checked me into the hospital and they ran a battery of tests and couldn't find anything wrong. Then they monitored it closely for the next three months and then for the next two years. At that point we sat down and wrote a letter to NASA and my doctor noted that the high bilirubin count was just an anomaly. It was like having six fingers on one hand or something.

"I reapplied for the space program and was selected for work in the Gemini missions. In fact, Buzz Aldrin and I both had high bilirubin counts. When Buzz and I flew in the Gemini 12 missions, it was known as the 'High Bilirubin Flight.'"

Fortunately for NASA and the rest of the crew on Apollo 13, Jim Lovell never let a little bilirubin keep him from living his dream of becoming an astronaut.

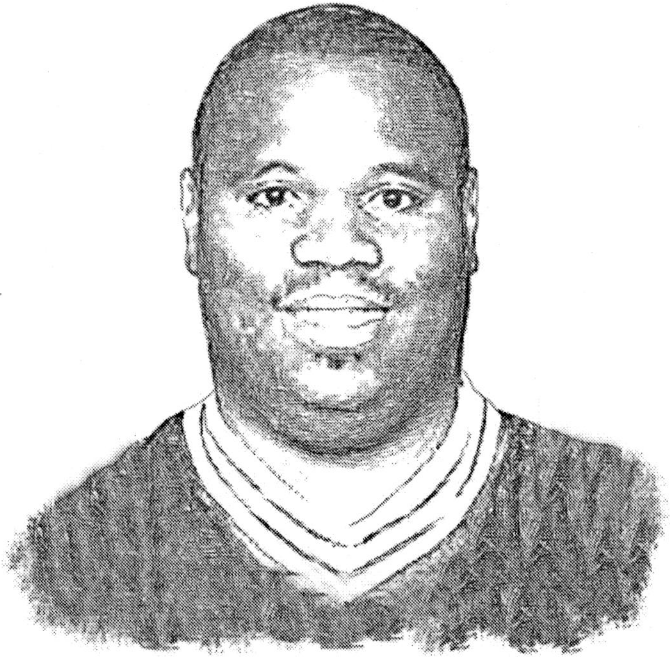

Russell Maryland

Man At Work

Russell Maryland has three Super Bowl rings. Was he the most talented player in the history of the NFL? No. But he was easily one of the hardest working players that the game has ever known. In this January, 1994 Sports Spectrum Magazine article, Maryland explains just a few of the reasons he was able to be successful in the world of professional football, where the average career is about three years and tales of "what might have been" are the rules rather than the exceptions.

Russell Maryland, the acknowledged Horatio Alger of the Dallas Cowboys, had not gotten a lot of playing time against Green Bay on this cloudy, overcast October day in Big D.

Dallas had won the game handily, largely on the strength of a five-field goal performance from kicker Eddie Murray. It was still early in the season and the win enabled the World Champion Cowboys to improve their record to 2-2.

Maryland, who hadn't started at defensive tackle because of a nagging foot injury he had sustained during the Cowboys' Super Bowl season, was not happy to be on the sidelines. He disdains anything that keeps him from going to work. In fact, he would probably play on both sides of the line if head coach Jimmy Johnson would let him.

"I just enjoy working hard," Maryland said, smiling despite his frustration. "I don't like to miss a down."

During the fall of 1992, while playing with a dislocated second toe on his left foot – an injury that required post-season surgery – Maryland was a major cog in the defensive wheel that helped Dallas roll to the NFL's top defensive rating. In their championship season, the Cowboys allowed less than 78 yards rushing per game on their way to a Super Bowl blowout of the Buffalo Bills. Maryland was a big part of that Super Bowl win, and it was largely because of Maryland that the "D" was back in Dallas.

"A lot of people think that success just happens overnight," Maryland said. "But it doesn't happen that way. Or at least it didn't happen that way for me. I had to work hard to get here, and I know I have to work harder if I want to stay here. I've had some problems with my feet this past summer and into the early season, and that's been a bit frustrating. I've never had the best feet in the NFL.

"Through it all, I've kept my faith in God. He has never left me, and even though life in the NFL can be extremely difficult, Jesus Christ constantly gives me strength to make it through another game or another day of two-a-days."

In high school, it was young Russell Maryland's parents who constantly kept him motivated. Not so much by what they said, but by what they did and how they did it.

"I grew up on the south side of Chicago," Maryland explains. "School was never really easy for me, but I always tried to work as hard as I could and usually made *A*'s. One of the reasons that I studied so hard was because of my parents. They were always working so hard. My father would leave for work before I got up in the morning and wouldn't get home until after I had gone to bed at night. He's a district manager for Chrysler Corporation in Chicago. My mother also worked hard at her job. She works for the city as an accountant for the police department. They had worked so hard to try to build a good life for me that I knew that I had to give something back to them. I wanted them to be proud of me, so I always worked as hard as I could at everything I did – whether it was academics or football or whatever."

After his academic achievements at prestigious Whitney Young High School in Chicago, Maryland could have easily gone to Yale or Harvard or any other Ivy League school. Instead, he decided to trade the cold winds of Chicago for tropical Miami, where he joined the Hurricanes and then-head coach Jimmy Johnson.

"It was really quite a shock to go down to Miami after being in Chicago all that time," Maryland said. "I was 17 years old and 1,500 miles away from home. I was so busy, though, that I really didn't have much time to be homesick."

Shortly after arriving in Miami, Maryland got a job at a local produce stand.

"I got a job down there selling produce because I needed some money," he recalls, before correcting himself. "Actually, I wasn't selling produce. I was washing it and doing some janitorial-type stuff. Kids have a tough time believing me when I say that, but I didn't mind. It was good, honest, work."

It was also hot work. Between that job and all the sprints that Maryland ran at Camp JJ, he lost 30 pounds during his first summer in Miami. By the time the year was over, he had dropped a total of 50 pounds from his original 6-1, 317-pound frame.

"Can you see me out there running those 100-yard dashes?" Maryland says, laughing. "There I was running just as hard as I could, all 317 pounds of me. I never finished first, but I never quit either."

After the grueling workouts, most of the team went back to their respective dorm rooms to take a nap. Maryland, however, could usually be found in the library after football practice.

"In college, there are so many distractions," Maryland explains. "And the problem is, there's nobody looking over your shoulder telling you that you have to study. As a result, you have to motivate yourself. There were a lot of times when I was tired and wanted to watch TV or sleep or whatever and just forget about going to the library. But I think the thing that kept me going was the fact that I didn't want to fail. I didn't want to disappoint my parents, and I didn't want to go back to Chicago a failure."

All the hard work paid off. Not only did Maryland receive a degree in psychology from the University of Miami, he was also the NFL's number one draft pick in 1991.

"There were a lot of people who said I'd never play in the NFL, much less be the number one pick in the country," Maryland said. "But I wanted to prove them wrong and also prove something to myself. All the things that I've accomplished in football and in academics couldn't have been accomplished if it weren't for my relationship with the Lord Jesus Christ. But I know that I have to do my part."

Super Bowl Memories
Super Bowl XXVII
January 31, 1993
Rose Bowl
Pasadena, California
Dallas Cowboys 52, Buffalo Bills 17

One of Russell Maryland's best memories from Super Bowl XXVII didn't happen on the field or in the locker room.

"Sure, it was great that we won the Super Bowl last year," Maryland said in 1994. "But my greatest Super Bowl memory was the chapel service at the hotel just prior to the game. We all got in a circle and held hands and prayed. Some of the players thanked God for the opportunity to play in such a big game, and others thanked God for their parents. The feeling I got from those few moments of prayer was just incredible.

"The verses that the chaplain spoke on that day were Ephesians 3:20,21, which say, 'Now to Him who is able to do immeasurably more than all we ask or imagine, according to His power that is at work within us, to Him be glory in church and in Christ Jesus throughout all generations, forever and ever! Amen.'

"When I thought about where the Cowboys were just four years ago and realized that on that day we were going to be playing for a world championship, it really made me realize how powerful God is and how much more He can do in my life if I'll only let Him."

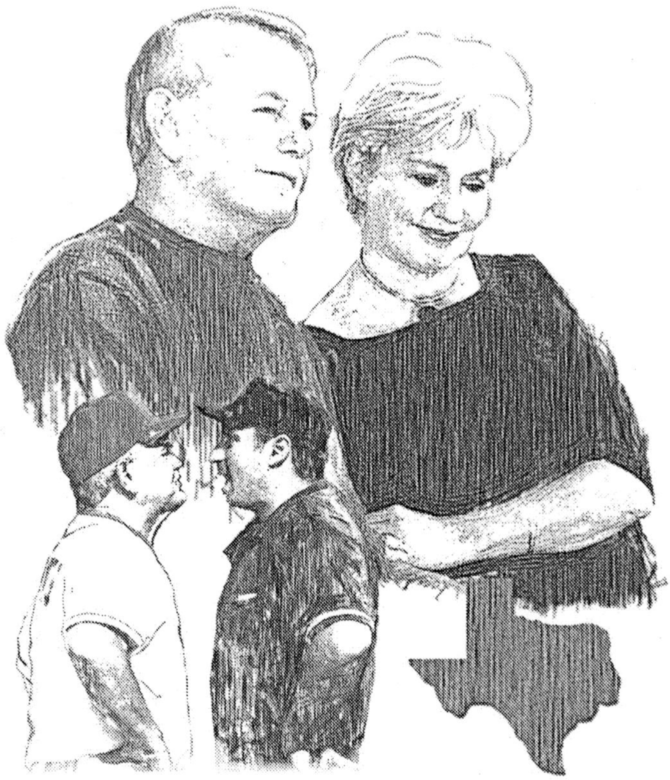

Johnny Oates

Deep in the Heart of Texas

It shouldn't be surprising that a number of the Heroes selected for this book have been fired from jobs they loved. Like Tony Dungy, Tom Landry and Dave Thomas, Johnny Oates was also unceremoniously fired. But, once he got to Texas, he did something that no other manager in Ranger history (including Ted Williams, Whitey Herzog and Billy Martin) was able to do – win an AL Western Division title. What we found in writing this book was that it's not where you start but where you finish. As this book went to press in the fall of 2004, Johnny Oates was battling brain cancer and fighting for his very life. When co-author John Weber visited with Oates at the Oates' home in Northern Virginia in early September, the former major league manager was still the eternal optimist. In fact, he was watching the Texas Rangers play the Minnesota Twins on satellite television. Thankful for the time that the Lord had given him, Oates seemed to have no regrets as he entered the final innings of his life. The stories below appeared in the July 1995 issue of Sports Spectrum Magazine, *when the biggest problem Oates had was the impending Major League Baseball strike. Johnny Oates went home to be with the Lord on December 24, 2004 at the age of 58.*

It was only a few weeks before the start of spring training. In a normal off-season, major league managers across the country would be gathered around the proverbial "Hot Stove League" to discuss a myriad of possible player transactions.

It was not, however, a normal off-season.

The owners had devised a plan to use replacement players instead of the regular players who had threatened to go on strike and the waver wires were buzzing. But not with the names of any players that you had ever heard of.

Before long, pitchers, catchers and plumbers had reported to spring training and the baseball world yawned a collective yawn.

Enter new Texas Rangers manager Johnny Oates who, amid all the confusion of a strike that seemed to have started sometime back in the Nixon era, remained one of the most positive people this side of Tommy Lasorda.

"I don't want this to be misinterpreted, and I don't want to sound as if I don't want the regular players to come back," Oates said at the time. "But my philosophy on this whole thing is that I've been hired by the Texas Rangers to manage this ball club and that's what I'm going to do. If the regular players come back, great. If not, then we're going to try to win as many games as we can with the people who do come out."

Of course, the regulars did come back, and Oates didn't have to go through the season trying to win a pennant with Rob Wishnevski, Lonnie Goldberg, Earl Wheeler and Gardner O'Flynn instead of Juan Gonzales, Will Clark, Ivan

Rodriquez and Kenny Rogers. But you get the idea that, either way, Oates would have said "Bring it on!"

"I really missed baseball last winter," Oates said. "I'm usually fired up and ready to go before the start of the season, but even more so this year because it has been so long. People are hungry to see baseball. I know I am. I went to Mexico in January just to see a baseball game. Our plane landed at 3 p.m. and we went straight to the ballpark. We didn't even check in at the hotel because I was so eager to see a game. Batting practice, infield, lights, hotdogs. It was great! And if it was that way for me, I can only imagine how the fans must have felt. They want to see baseball."

If Oates is anything, he is an optimist.

His wife Gloria knew early in the spring that her husband was ready for baseball, no matter what happened with the negotiations.

"Johnny called me early in March," she recalls, "and told me he already had an opening day lineup ready to go if the strike wasn't settled by April. He really is unbelievable. He's determined to make the best of any situation he's faced with, and I think that's why he's been so successful over the years."

Former Ranger first baseman Rafael Palmeiro, who played for Oates in Baltimore last year, suggests another reason. Players like playing for Oates, Palmeiro said, because they always know where they stand with him.

"Johnny treats players with respect," Palmeiro said. "Because he respects you, it's easy to respect him. He is a good family man. His family comes first. You don't see that too often in baseball. He values the things that are really important. His values are where they need to be. He is great to play for and to work with."

Palmeiro recalled an incident from the spring of 1994 that spoke volumes about Oates the man, if not the manager.

"You could always tell that Johnny had his priorities in the right order," Palmeiro said. "My wife needed to catch a plane early one morning to return home when we were at spring training. The day before her plane left, I asked Johnny if I could be a little late to practice the next day. He told me to take care of my family first. They always come before baseball. A lot of coaches say things like that, but you knew that Johnny always meant it."

Palmeiro played for Oates for only one season and that season was short-lived because of the 1994 baseball strike.

At the time Baltimore owner Peter Angelos dismissed Oates after a strike-shortened 1994 campaign, the former Oriole catcher had guided his old club to a mark well above .500 and had the club hovering at or near first place for most of the season.

But Angelos's style clashed with Oates's, and soon Oates found himself at odds with the O's owner.

"Last year was a tough year for me, but I wouldn't trade it for anything in the world," Oates said. "God taught me so much through all the adversity that I went through up in Baltimore. At the time, I hated going through it. But now, looking back, I see how God used that time in my life to make me a stronger person."

Oates smiles when he thinks back to 1994.

"I've given the 1994 season a lot of thought over the past several months, and there's no doubt in my mind that the Lord is not going to give me anything that I can't handle with His help if I allow Him to help me," Oates said. "My problem was that I was trying to handle it myself, and I just kept fighting it. I was going to do it *my* way. It was one of those summers where the Lord really just had to get my attention before I woke up.

"It just seemed like it was a year where, even though we were winning, things just weren't going that well. There was a misunderstanding about who should play and who should not play. I went home on a Thursday for my son's graduation, and when I returned on Friday there was the article in the paper about me being a bad leader and a bad manager," he said.

"It all seemed to be snowballing as we went into New York for a series against the Yankees. I got thrown out of a ballgame in that series, and as I went up the tunnel in Yankee Stadium, I got a feeling that is just impossible to describe. No one who hasn't experienced it can really understand it.

"I sat down in that tunnel and I could hear the crowd out there in this old, dark part of the stadium. I just said, 'Lord, come and help me!' At that moment, I let my job go. I had been holding my job with a closed fist saying, 'I'm not going to let this thing go!' I had put something that was temporary as number one.

"My vocation and my job are temporary. Jesus is forever and eternal. I was clinging to something so strongly, and it was as if the Lord was saying, 'John, nothing is going to be right until you let go of this job. Turn it over to Me and I'll take care of it for you."

Soon, Oates was out of Baltimore and on his way to Texas, where he would lead the Rangers to their first AL West title.

EXTRA INNINGS

Few people in baseball know Johnny Oates as well as Ranger GM Doug Melvin does. Their friendship dates back more than 15 years, when both men were with the Yankees.

"When Johnny was catching for the Yankees, I was a batting practice pitcher and kept charts for the team," Melvin said. "He had been released by the Dodgers in March of 1980 and then signed by the Yankees the next month. When our starting catcher would need a day off, Johnny would come in and get a key hit or throw somebody out. He was always a role player who watched the game and studied how it was played."

Melvin added that part of Oates' success stems from hard work.

"Johnny has such a solid work ethic," Melvin says. "He still gets on the airplane and reads the rulebook, even though he has read it a hundred times. He's very meticulous, very organized. You go into his office and everything is all very orderly. He puts his pen in a certain spot and his notes in a certain spot, and that's a lot different from a lot of people. But these are some things that make him such a great manager."

~ ~ ~ ~ ~ ~

CHAIRMAN OF THE JOINT CHIEFS OF STAFF
WASHINGTON, D.C. 20318-0001

21 August 1992

Mr. Jim Gibbs
Apartment 2008
2207 Cornerstone Lane
Arlington, Texas 76013

Dear Mr. Gibbs,

Thank you for your recent letter informing me of your "Heroes" book project. I truly appreciate your interest and the kind words.

Youth are the future of our Nation and I take every opportunity to share my experiences growing up in the South Bronx with young people. I always stress the importance of hard work, striving to do one's very best, setting goals, having a vision, not doing drugs and taking advantage of the many resources available to them. I wish it were possible for me to discuss these values with you and contribute to your feature story. Unfortunately, because I will be on leave for the remainder of August and the fact that there are so many outstanding similar requests which I must honor before taking on any new commitments, I must decline your gracious offer.

Although I am unable to grant you an interview, I am enclosing several articles, speeches, biographies, photographs, and a videotape entitled, "General Powell Talks to Young People." I hope this material will be helpful background information. Should you require additional details, Mrs. Joan Asboth in my Public Affairs Office will be happy to assist you. She may be reached at (703) 697-4272.

With best wishes for a successful and rewarding project.

Sincerely,

COLIN L. POWELL
Chairman
of the
Joint Chiefs of Staff

Colin Powell

Back in the Bronx

Unfortunately, Colin Powell was the only person we didn't get to personally interview for this book. But, as you can see from the enclosed letter, he was certainly more than willing to help us out with our Heroes project. When we contacted him in 1992, he had just retired as the Chairman of the Joint Chiefs of Staff and was busy writing his own autobiography. As this book went to press in early October of 2004, Powell was still serving his country admirably and still working hard at his position as U.S. Secretary of State under President George W. Bush. The story below was written with the help of videos and other information provided by Powell and his staff. The authors salute President Bush and General Powell as well as the thousands of U.S. troops who are fighting abroad so that we can have peace and freedom at home.

He had come back to Morris High School in New York for the first time in 37 years on this cloudy, April day of 1991. He had left there as a *C* student in 1954 with a high school diploma and now, some 37 years later, he was retiring as

General Colin L. Powell, Chairman of the Joint Chiefs of Staff.

It's been said that a person cannot go back home again, yet Powell was here, one of the few who had made it, talking to hundreds of students at his old high school.

At age 52, Powell was the youngest Chairman in the history of the office, which was created in 1949 by an amendment to the National Security Act of 1947. He was also the first African-American to hold the Chairmanship, the most senior and prestigious of positions in the American military.

Yes, he had come a long way from those humble beginnings in the South Bronx and now he was back where it all began, almost four decades from the time he had started.

Powell related to a packed Morris High gymnasium that, as he passed the place where his old home used to be on 952 Kelly St. that day, a flood of old memories came rushing back.

"That trip brought back memories of four years of coming down three flights of steps, going up Kelly Street, down Westchester, along Intervale, over the hill crossing Prospect, up Longwood, up 166th and then into Morris High for four years of education, and now I return 37 years later as Chairman of the Joint Chiefs of Staff," Powell said.

"In case you don't know what the Chairman of the Joint Chiefs of Staff really means, or what my job is, I am military advisor to the President of the United States and the Secretary of Defense and the National Security Council," he said. "I'm responsible for the three million active and reserve GIs who are serving their nation around the world."

Powell will be the first to tell you that his was not an easy job. During Operation Desert Storm, he made hundreds of split-second decisions during the course of any given day

Real American Heroes

as advisor to President Bush. Along the way, there was the Korean War, two tours of duty in Vietnam where he was fired upon, had a steel spike driven through his foot and survived numerous other battle scars. His military career has included commanding more than a million troops on the U.S. mainland. He has pulled men out of burning helicopters and has literally put his life on the line for his country more times than he could probably count during his 30-plus years in the U.S. Army.

His Chairman's office at the Pentagon in Washington was a long way from Morris High School in New York. And students, it seems, always want to know how Powell rose through the ranks and became the first black Chairman of the Joint Chiefs of Staff.

"People always want to know how I got to this position," Powell continued. "And that is a difficult question to answer because a lot of things go into that answer. But I know where it all started. It started the day in 1954 when I got a diploma from Morris High School. That diploma opened doors for me, it led me to college at City College of New York and from college to the Army and, after entering the army, 33 years of a very satisfying and happy career."

It was at that point that Powell drove the point home to students at his old high school.

"The point I want to make to you this morning, not-withstanding the lights and the microphones, is that if you finish high school and get that diploma, you are on your way to somewhere. It may mean becoming a general. It may mean becoming a teacher. It might mean becoming a politician or a businessman or a lawyer or an accountant.

"But if you finish high school and you get that diploma, you are on your way somewhere, even though you don't know where that somewhere is, even though there may be tough roads ahead as you go on out. But you are on your way to somewhere."

The opposite of that, Powell added, is also true.

"If you don't get that high school diploma, you're on your way to nowhere. You're on your way to the dead end. In fact, if you don't get that high school diploma, you probably can't even get into the army these days. You look at the army right now and over 97 percent of the GIs who are serving have their high school diploma.

"We like high school graduates in our armed forces for a very simple reason. We know when we take somebody in who is a high school graduate, we have somebody who is able to stick with it. Somebody who has demonstrated a commitment. Somebody who has overcome obstacles and challenges. Somebody who we can then counsel on being a good soldier or sailor or airman or marine."

Besides stressing the importance of getting a high school diploma, Powell also made it clear to the hundreds of students at his old high school that experimenting with illegal drugs is not the smart thing to do.

"When I was coming along and about your age, we had problems, too," he said. "We had drugs in our neighborhood. It isn't something that has just come along in the last couple of years. We had lots of drugs in my neighborhood. On every street corner there was some pothead or junkie who was trying to sell or deal or get others involved in it.

"I didn't do it. Never in my life, not even to experiment, not to try, not to see what it would be like. For two reasons. One, my parents would have killed me, but the second reason is that somewhere along the line I and a couple of my friends, one of whom is here now - Gene Norman, who grew up on Kelly Street -- knew it was stupid. It was stupid. It was the most self-destructive thing you could do with the life that

God and your parents had given to you. The use of drugs was stupid and we didn't do it."

Those who did do it, Powell said, have suffered the consequences.

"Of all the kids that I grew up with on Kelly Street, Gene Norman, one or two others, made it. Too many of the others did not make it. They went to jail, where they died, or were never heard from again."

Fortunately for the U.S. Armed Forces, Colin Powell did make it. This speech at Morris High School is just one of hundreds of speeches that Powell gives to kids of all ages during the course of a given year. From Morris High School in New York City, to Hudson Bay High School in Vancouver, Washington to Fisk University in Nashville, Tennessee, Powell is one of the most sought-after speakers in the United States today.

He is a four-star general, the U.S. Armed forces highest ranking officer and, largely because of his success as top military advisor to [the first] President Bush during Operation Desert Storm, a celebrity in his own right.

In a speech to a group of youngsters in Boys Town, Nebraska, Powell pondered the question of whether he had always aspired to be the nation's number one G.I. Joe.

"I have a very important and responsible position," he said. "And, in recent years, people have been asking me, 'Gosh, you're a four-star general. When you were a young boy coming up in the South Bronx did you know, did you ever dream, could you have ever imagined that one day you would be a four-star general and that you would be Chairman of the Joint Chiefs of Staff?'"

"And the answer I give them is 'Yeah, sure.' There I was – eight-, nine-, 10-years old in the streets of New York City playing stickball, running from cops because they used to chase us. Because, by the way, the way you got a stickball bat was to steal somebody's broom and cut off the handle and that was your bat. And the cops were forever chasing us.

"And when those cops chased me through the alleys, I used to say to myself 'I can't wait until I grow up and become a four-star general and get away from all this.'"

The students laughed. Actually, Powell didn't know what he wanted to be when he grew up. In fact, he will be the first to tell you that, as a youngster in elementary school, he wasn't a very good student.

"When I was in the fourth grade, they put me in the slow learners' class," he said. "They said, 'There's something wrong with you. We're going to put you back for a while until we can figure out what it is and bring you along.'"

Throughout elementary school, junior high and high school, Powell's grades were mediocre. Somewhere along the line, though, he realized what he needed to do to become successful.

"You have to know what this country is all about," he said. "You have to be able to read and you have to be able to communicate with people. I understood that, above all, I had to stay in long enough to get a high school diploma."

Even more importantly, Powell realized how important it is to respect others. A high school diploma may be the first step, he said, but if you don't respect other people, you may also be on your way to nowhere.

"When I was in elementary school, I learned the importance of respecting people. Loving one another, caring for one another. And, if you do that, you will find that others will treat you in the same way," he said.

He also learned to have confidence in himself.

"I also learned to always, always, believe in myself," he said. "I have always believed that, to a certain extent, my fate has always been in my own hands. I never let what others thought about me become my problem. I'm a black man. I was a black kid. But for me, I used that blackness as a source of pride, a source of inspiration. I never let it become my problem. I always made it someone else's problem but not mine.

"So whatever makes you different, whether it's your color or your race or your religion or your family background or a handicap that you might have, use it as a source of pride. Use it as a source of strength. Use it as a source of getting ahead in the world. Let no one or no thing hold you back. Always believe in your heart that you can succeed, that you can do anything that you want to do. And then work for it and never stop working for it."

And work for it Powell did. Born in Harlem to Jamaican immigrants who labored in Manhattan's garment district, Powell grew up in the impoverished South Bronx. His childhood home has since been burned out by drug dealers and has undergone numerous changes since he was a boy. Life growing up was obviously not easy for Powell.

Yet, Powell is a man who will seldom complain about his childhood. His parents may not have had a lot of money and he may have gone to ROTC at New York City College instead of West Point, but he will be the first to tell you that he was very blessed as a child.

"I had a great childhood," he told one reporter. "I had a close family that provided everything that I needed."

Powell said that, growing up, he got a lot of the values that he has today from his parents.

"We didn't sit around and talk about values like the Brady Bunch or anything like that," he told Ed Bradley of *60 Minutes*. "I just watched my parents and learned from them.

They were good people and they passed those values down to me."

Indeed it was Powell's parents who, probably without realizing it, gave young Colin the desire to always do his best at whatever he was going to do.

"My parents, like so many parents of City College of New York students, were immigrants," Powell wrote in the college's alumnus magazine. "They came to this country in the 1920s and worked their entire adult lives in the garment district - my father as a sales clerk, my mother as a seamstress. I recall that every Thursday night I would watch my mother put those little tickets together - she did piecework - so that on Friday morning she could bundle them all up and take them down to 34th Street and get her pay.

"You were supposed to do better than that in my family and, I think, in most of the families of those who attended CCNY in those days. Indeed, the parental drive in that direction was so strong that our parents didn't recognize their own strengths. Until the day they died, for example, I was never able to convince my parents that it would never be possible for me to do better than they did in providing their children with values and goals and, in that way, they were making a valuable contribution to their new country, which they loved."

On this cloudy overcast day in the South Bronx, Colin Powell made it clear that he too loves his country. He also showed a packed gymnasium at Morris Town High that even a *C* student can come back home again.

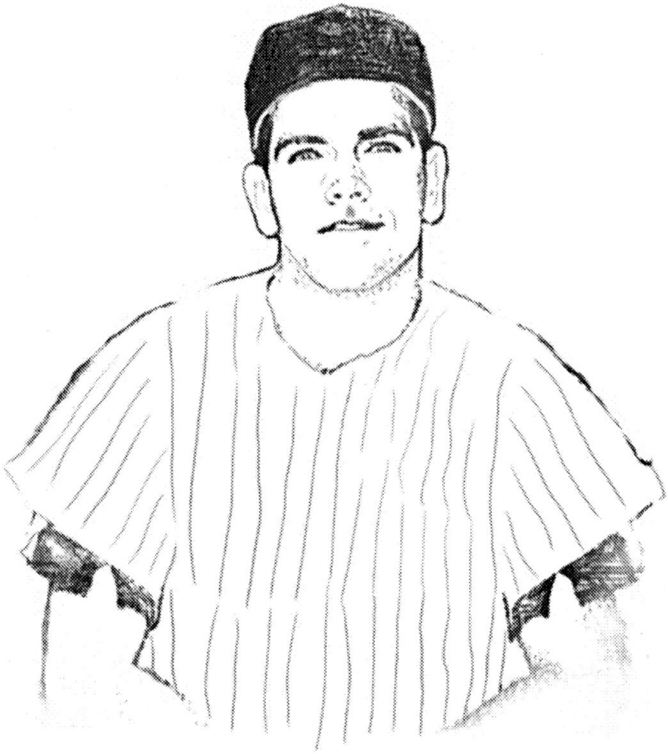

Bobby Richardson

Winter Meeting

Bill Mazeroski may have hit the home run that beat the New York Yankees and made the Pittsburgh Pirates world champions in 1960. But sportswriters still selected Yankee second baseman Bobby Richardson as the World Series MVP that year. We met Richardson at the Major League Baseball Winter Meetings in Louisville, Kentucky back in 1992. We had both grown up idolizing Richardson as much for his strong Christian faith as we did for his skills on the baseball field. What we found when we interviewed him was that he was as sincere in person as he was when we saw him turn a double play on TV or writing to his fans in his autobiography - The Bobby Richardson Story. *The story that appears below was written shortly after the Major League Baseball strike of 1994 but the actual time setting for the story is 1992.*

The sun was shining brightly on this cold December day in Louisville, Kentucky but it was apparent that the 1992 Major League Baseball Winter Meetings would have a decidedly different tone than the previous year's meetings in Miami.

Two years later, owners and players would reach an impasse that would lead to a strike that eventually caused the World Series to be canceled. In 1992, the division between players and owners widened and, as time would later tell, foreshadow the 1994 strike.

Bobby Richardson, however, remained at peace with the whole situation. At the time, Richardson was president of Baseball Chapel and knew a large number of the players and how the threat of a work stoppage would hurt everyone, not to mention casting a cloud over our National Past Time. Still, he seemed to say, God is in control.

Baseball negotiations, like the weather, are out of his jurisdiction.

"It's a little colder here than it was in Miami last year," said Richardson as he pulled his small rental car out on to a long strip of Kentucky highway that led to this year's [1992] meetings. "I'm looking forward to going to the convention, though. It's been a while since I've been to Louisville."

The weather and tropical Miami was not the only thing that was different about these particular winter meetings in December of 1992. Baseball owners had fired their commissioner and the owners, slowly coming to grips with the fact that TV revenue was drying up and that players' salaries were skyrocketing, were talking about a lockout in spring training.

"It is a time we should really be praying for baseball," said someone in the back of the car.

At that point, Richardson smiled quietly. The smile seemed to say that everything would be okay. And, if indeed there was a lockout, that the grand old game of baseball would somehow still survive despite the best efforts of those who would foul it up.

It is that type of attitude, the approach that God is indeed in control, that makes Richardson just as popular in baseball circles today as he was when he was named Most Valuable Player of the 1960 World Series. It has now been more than 26 years since he retired from baseball at the ripe old age of 31 in 1966. Still, inside the crowded convention hall near the Gault House Hotel in downtown Louisville, Richardson meets few strangers.

Tommy Tresh and Andy Carey, both teammates of Richardson in New York, now have baseball related businesses and, over the years, have become regulars at these winter meetings. Both are glad to see Richardson and both are just two examples of the many friends that Richardson has made over the years.

It is no secret to anybody who knows Bobby Richardson that he is a strong Christian who loves his Lord. He prays before meals at restaurants and never hesitated to share the Gospel of Christ with his teammates when he played for the Yankees. Now, as president of Baseball Chapel, his Christian influence is even greater, although Bobby himself will be the first to tell you that actions speak louder than words.

"When it comes to sharing the Gospel of Jesus Christ, you first have to earn the right to speak to people," he said from a quiet corner of the convention floor later that day. "Let's take the New York Yankees, for example. We were a ball club that traveled around together everywhere. Twenty-five fellows on a bus, a plane, a train. All in the same hotel together. Now, if you've got someone who is going to try to collar you all the time, you are going to move away from him. And I think my idea was that I wanted to be available for people.

"I just let people know that, 'Hey, the Lord is real in my life and I want to be available if you want to talk to me.' And on many occasions, traveling, that's exactly what would happen. They'd come over and sit down and we would have long visits about the Lord or about various other things. In later years after my retirement, I've had several of my teammates that would call me up and we'd just visit for a little bit. Roger Maris' wife called me and wanted me to represent the Yankees at Roger's funeral. I did the Eulogy at his funeral and also at Dick Howser's (former Yankee and Royal manager) funeral as well. So there was a real rapport that, over the years, has continued.

"Right now, we're together at the winter meetings and I can walk down the aisle and see Tommy Tresh or Andy Carey or whoever it might be and there's a real rapport that I still have. And I feel that's important in witnessing. I feel like you have to earn the right and I feel like you can't represent one thing if your life doesn't bare it out. You can't just say, 'Well, this is how it should be done. I don't do it this way, but this is how it should be done.' Being a good example goes a long way in helping win people to Christ."

Just one of those who was influenced by Richardson's example is former Yankee infielder Andy Carey, who had already played with the Yankees for a number of seasons by the time Richardson won a permanent spot on the Yankees' roster in 1957. Carey said he was impressed with how the young man from South Carolina handled himself on the baseball field but, more importantly, he was also impressed with how easily Richardson made friends with his new teammates.

"He was very religious, yet he never made any of us feel uncomfortable," Carey said. "He and Tony Kubek were good friends and neither of them ever drank. There were a lot of times when a big group of us would all be out together and they'd be having a soda pop while the rest of us would be drinking beer. The great thing about Bobby is that he never had a holier than thou attitude toward anyone and people could always respect him. I think that's why he was so popular with our teammates when we were playing and also why they're always so glad to see him today at old timer's games and different things like that."

In 1966, after both men had finished their playing careers, Richardson spoke to a group of people in Los Angeles. Carey, who was in town for a World Series game between the Los Angeles Dodgers and the Baltimore Orioles, was in the audience. When Richardson gave the invitation for those who did not know Christ to accept Him as their personal Savior, Carey came forward.

"I'll never forget that day," he said. "When Bobby shared his testimony and then gave the invitation, I couldn't help but remember his great example when we were together with the Yankees. He was always a first-class guy and suddenly, on that day in 1966, I realized that I needed to accept Christ as my Savior."

Today [1992], Carey, in addition to his successful insurance business, is also the Executive Director of The Drug-Free MI-Stars Foundation, a group dedicated to keeping kids away from drugs and alcohol.

Just as Richardson is patient when it comes to knowing when to share the Gospel of Christ with others, he was also patient as a player.

"In those days, guys didn't play at a young age, particularly with the New York Yankees." Carey said. "Bobby was always one of the hardest working guys on the team, yet he knew that he was going to have to be patient to break into our lineup. You've got to remember that the Yankees were going to the

World Series almost every year during the 1950s and early 1960s when Bobby and I played. Most of the guys on our bench could have been starters on other ball clubs. That's why I have such great respect for Bobby. He just kept working hard, waiting for his turn. Patience is the key to success in a lot of areas of life and no one seemed to exemplify that more than Bobby."

When his break finally did come, Richardson was ready. Stops in cities like Norfolk, Olean, Binghamton, Denver and Richmond had prepared him well and, by 1957, he had won a spot on the Yankee roster. By 1959, he had put in a solid season for the Bronx Bombers, playing in 134 games and batting over .300 for the first time in his career.

In 1960, Richardson appeared in 150 games for the Yanks and, while his season batting average dropped slightly, he more than made up for it with one of the most spectacular performances in World Series history.

He started every game of that seven-game World Series against the Pittsburgh Pirates, coming to bat 30 times and batting .367. He collected 11 hits, drove in 12 runs and also had a grand slam home run.

During the regular season in 1960, Richardson, not known for the long ball, had only one home run and 26 RBI during a course of 150 games and 460 at bats.

Suddenly, in just seven games and 30 at bats in the 1960 World Series, Richardson had hit a grand slam homer and had driven in 12 runs, almost half of his RBI total for the whole year.

"It's really funny how that particular home run [the grand slam] came about because I was batting eighth that day and the bases were loaded and Whitey Ford was pitching," Richardson said. "I think we had already scored about three runs that day, and in a situation like that during the season,

Stengel would often pinch hit for me and I was listening for him to call my name. 'Hold that gun!' is what he usually said. But he didn't say anything this time. Then I realized why. He had me bunting. Now that's not a good play in baseball, to bunt with the bases loaded, but he wanted me to get one more run in and then maybe Whitey could drive in another one.

"Well, I fouled the ball off twice and then Frank Crossetti, one of our coaches, told me to hit the ball to right field and stay out of the double play. I was trying to do that and the ball was inside. I was able to get around on it and the ball went out of the park! I was just as surprised as anybody in the stands. It was the only home run I had hit in post-season play. In fact that year, I only hit one home run. I only had 26 RBIs that year but I had 12 in that World Series. Baseball is a funny game the way things happen like that. But I was fortunate in that I played in so many World Series games. I played in 30 consecutive World Series games, which is a nice streak, but I think I just played at the right time."

Richardson won the Most Valuable Player Award for the 1960 World Series, but the Pirates eventually won the series on Bill Mazeroski's dramatic game-winning homer in Game Seven.

During Richardson's career, the Yankees went to the World Series seven times and he appeared in 36 games, batting a solid .305 after collecting 40 hits in 131 at bats in the Fall Classic.

Not bad for a guy that many said was too small to play Major League Baseball.

"That was something that I heard all of my life," Richardson said. "But, to be honest, it never really bothered me a whole lot. One of my idols growing up was Phil Rizzuto and I knew I was bigger than he was so, when they would say something like that, I would just ignore it. I think baseball is the one sport where there are so many ways you can compensate. You can learn to be a good bunter, you can hit the ball behind the runner, you can steal bases. There are other things that you can do that can compensate for that size which will give you more power and allow you to hit the long ball or throw harder."

So, in order to make the big leagues, Bobby knew that he had to not only work harder than players who were bigger than he was, he also had to develop the skills he was blessed with such as his speed and his outstanding defensive skills.

"The thing that I remember about growing up in Sumter as an eight- or nine-year old boy was that times were different in those days and sports were a very big part of my life," he said. "Sumter was like a lot of communities at that time in that they had Little League baseball. It wasn't called Little League baseball; it was called Knee Pants League and my father had always wanted me to play baseball. He had played some but had to work and couldn't follow through with his dreams of becoming a big leaguer so he afforded me all the opportunities of playing at the Little League level.

"I just engrossed myself in playing baseball. I'd have a friend come over and we would play catch. When my dad would come home in the evenings, we would play catch. We would play pepper with each other, we would jump the school fence to get on the baseball field so we could play and it just seemed like my whole life centered around baseball. And basketball. I had a goal in my back yard and my friends would come over and we would shoot baskets. At that time, sports just dominated my life. I enjoyed it very much. I don't think I stood out, but I just loved it so much and was just so active that I eventually got pretty good at them."

In fact, it was Richardson's love for sports that eventually got him out of what he now refers to as "a shy stage" of his life.

"I can remember that I didn't want to go to school when I was a kid," he said. "And I went through a period in about the first or second grade where I lived just a block away from the school. We usually walked to school and there was a policeman who would help us cross the street. For some reason, growing up, I just didn't enjoy school. Didn't want to go. I'd get there and come up with a toothache or an earache or for some reason not feel well enough to stay. There were a lot of days when I would get back home from school before my dad left for work. It was embarrassing in the sense that it was embarrassing to my folks.

"I don't remember one moment where I, personally, was embarrassed. But I do know that it was nice to get over that and I think that sports played a big part in helping me get over that. I started enjoying going to school and I couldn't wait for recess to come and then, after school, I'd stay and play ball. So it worked out all right."

Like many boys growing up today, Richardson lived in a quiet rural area and his father's business didn't exactly lend itself to a lot of social activities.

"I was very shy as a boy," he said. "My father was in the tombstone business - marble and granite - and didn't travel very much. As a young boy growing up, other than sports, we didn't do a whole lot. On Sunday afternoons we would drive out to the cemetery and then Dad would take a carbon copy of a stone that he was asked to duplicate. I think I was just not used to the social aspects of growing up and was just very much on the shy side."

Every generation has its share of problems and temptations and, even in small communities like Sumter,

South Carolina, it is still hard to get away from things like peer pressure and other obstacles that take young people away from the Lord, Richardson said.

"I think peer pressure is a tremendous distraction now," he added. "What you've got to realize is that, particularly in our public school system, you've got situations where these young kids who may come out of a church background with Christian parents are suddenly in situations where they're with kids who will try to get them to do things that are not right. The temptations that come through peer pressure are tremendous at an early age and, later, when you look down the road at things like drugs and alcohol, the temptations are even worse. The young people growing up today have it so much tougher in that area than we did. They have temptations that just abound from every direction."

The problem, however, is that peer pressure is not just something that young people go through. Many adults go through the same thing every day. Part of overcoming peer pressure as an adult, Richardson said, is locking into strong values at a young age.

"One of the reasons I was able to overcome peer pressure to drink or smoke or do things I shouldn't do when I was with the Yankees was that I had the respect of my teammates," he said. "Number one, I had the respect of my teammates. There were several occasions where one of my teammates would use some foul language and say, 'Oh Bobby, I'm sorry. I didn't see you.' And he'd just move right on down the line. Well, I think what they realized was that I wasn't condemning them or thought I was better than them. That wasn't there at all. I just think they realized that I knew I shouldn't use that language and that, all of a sudden when they were around me, that they shouldn't either. So the rapport was there and no doors were closed so that I might have the chance on any occasion to share the Lord with them."

TV can also have a negative influence, Richardson said.

"Personally, I think television is one of the biggest distractions kids have today," he said. "You can turn on any television set today and, because of the money involved, and the various things involved to sponsor an athletic event or whatever it might be, there are temptations that were just not around during the time I was growing up. I know out of the group that I ran around with, drinking was not a problem, smoking was not a problem and there again it all just centered around sports – one-on-one in basketball, touch football in the back yard and, of course, baseball. But today's young boy or girl growing up just has so much more to deal with. Not only from television, but also from the way our society has gone.

"Things have turned around. When I was growing up, we would have prayer and devotionals in our classrooms with our teachers and now it is impossible to do that. I just think that the way our country is going just makes it very difficult for young people to take a stand."

Yet in his quiet way, Richardson has taken a stand. Three months later, in the bright sunshine of Arizona and Florida, baseball is alive once again. The December talk of lockouts and a delayed season has now given way to games of pepper and extra batting practice.

As Robert Clinton Richardson will be the first to tell you, baseball is always bigger than the people who try to foul it up.

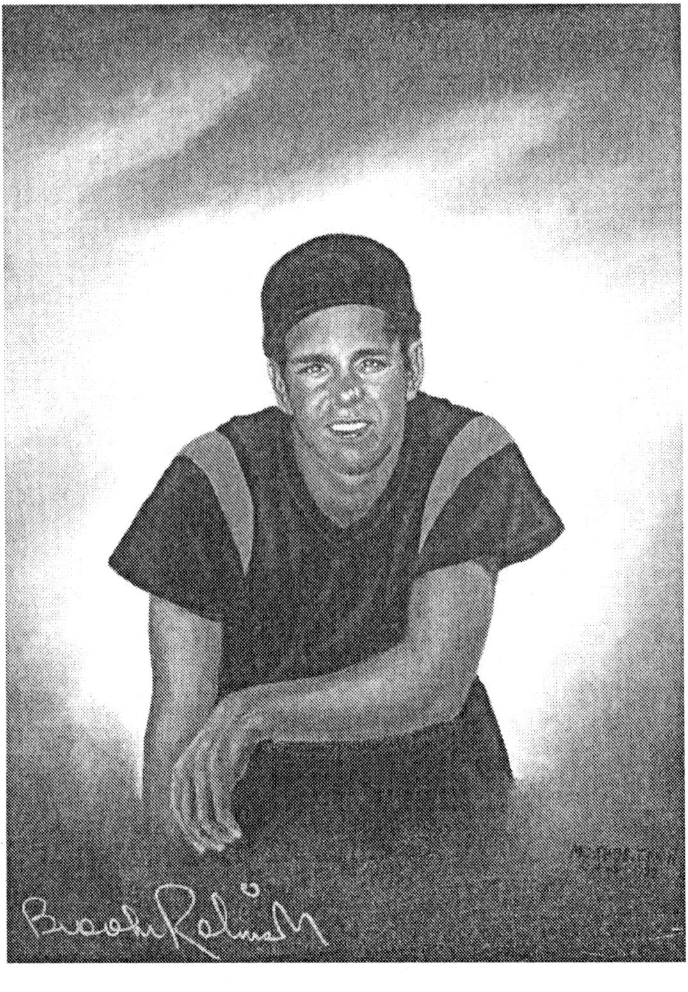

Brooks Robinson

Oriole Magic

Looking back, this book may have gotten its start in April of 1977 when co-author Jim Gibbs met Brooks Robinson at a toy store in Fort Worth, Texas. It's interesting for us to think back to that time in the late 1970s as we go to press with this book in October of 2004. Professional Sports and professional athletes have changed so radically since that day that the story below almost seems like a fairy tale. Nobody charging for autographs. No rude public relations people trying to order people around. Just Brooks and a few of his fans on a rainy day at Bolen's Toy Palace in Fort Worth, a few miles from where the Baltimore Orioles would play the Texas Rangers later that evening. Twenty-three autographs? No problem, Jim. The story below was written by co-author Jim Gibbs while he was a student at the University of Texas in 1983 shortly after he returned from Cooperstown, N.Y., where he saw Robinson inducted into the National Baseball Hall of Fame.

It was a rainy day in April of 1977 and Brooks Robinson was in what turned out to be his last season with the Baltimore Orioles. I was in eighth grade that year and my all-time favorite baseball player was going to be making an appearance at a toy store in Fort Worth, Texas which was about 60 miles north of my hometown of Glen Rose, Texas.

Doug DeCinces had replaced Brooks as the O's regular third baseman at mid-season the year before, but to me and Oriole fans across the country, it didn't seem to matter. Third base still belonged to Brooks Calbert Robinson Jr. just as it had since 1955, when Robinson played his first game there.

The rain had kept most fans at home that day but there was nothing that could have kept me away from Bolin's Toy Palace in Fort Worth on that rainy, spring day in 1977. Sure, I had school just like every other kid did that day but my mom knew how much I wanted to go see Brooks so she explained it all to my eighth grade English teacher, Becky Ice, who let me out of class so that we could make the drive up to Fort Worth to see Brooks.

Brooks signed 23 autographs for me that day and, while he amiably obliged, my mom was capturing it all on film.

"Get a shot of me and the Ol' Master," I remember saying.

"'The Old Master?'" Brooks repeated laughing. "Wait a minute, Jim! I'm not *that* old!"

Today, Brooks is just as popular as he ever has been as it has been more than six years since that rainy day in Fort Worth, Texas. Instead of being in eighth grade at Bolin's Toy Palace in Fort Worth, I'm now a junior at the University of Texas and am in Cooperstown, New York to see Brooks get inducted into the National Baseball Hall of Fame.

Oh sure, Juan Marichal, George Kell and Walter Alston are all being inducted as well, but somehow this overcast day in Cooperstown seems to belong to Brooks Calbert Robinson Jr., "The Human Vacuum Cleaner."

More than two planes and 50 buses had come from Baltimore to see Brooks, and Cooperstown, a small town of about 2,300, had suddenly been transformed into a national convention of the Brooks Robinson Fan Club.

After Brooks made his speech and the ceremonies were completed, Brooks and other inductees were whisked off into the Hall of Fame Library and driven back to their hotel.

The next day, two hours before the scheduled start of the annual Hall of Fame game between the Orioles and St. Louis Cardinals, it was raining hard as I sat in my rental car about 10 blocks from Doubleday Field, reading about the induction ceremonies in the local newspaper and wondering whether or not the game would be rained out.

After an hour, the skies cleared and I began to make my way down town. About a half block from the car, I remembered my camera. Something told me that I would need it.

As I walked past the hotel where all the inductees were staying, I decided to go down and see what was going on. Bill Dickey, the New York Yankee great, and Al Lopez, who both played and managed in the big leagues, were on the porch at that hotel and while I got their autographs and took pictures, I talked with Lopez about Debs Garms, a former teammate of his who now lives in my hometown of Glen Rose, Texas.

In the lobby, I noticed Brooks' brother Gary and his family. I knew it was only a matter of time before Brooks would be down to join them.

Finally, Brooks came out and I got a few pictures and shook hands with him. A 10-year-old boy with an Oriole cap on also had his camera ready.

"Can I have a picture, Mr. Robinson?" the boy asked.

"Sure," Brooks said. "Wait a minute," he added, taking off his sunglasses and bending down.

The boy went over by Brooks while his mom took the picture, more than six years after my own mom had taken a picture of me with "The Ol' Master."

Brooks then made his way out to a van in the hotel parking lot.

"Who was that?" asked the boy's six-year-old sister.

"That was a Hall of Famer," the boy answered.

"Yes," I thought, a Hall of Famer in every sense of the word.

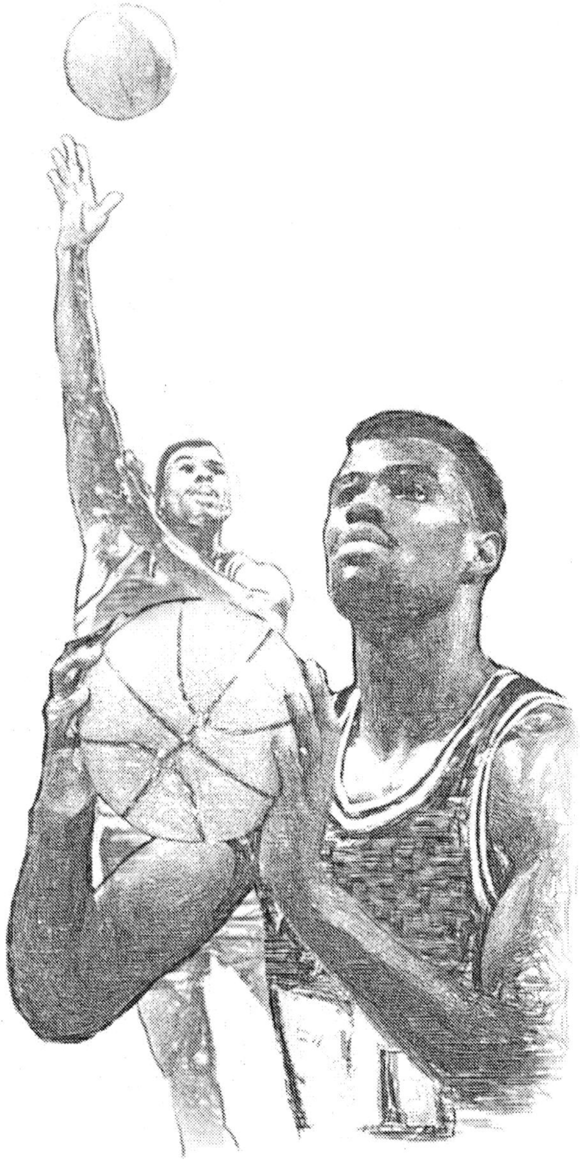

David Robinson

Mr. Robinson's Neighborhood

When we met David Robinson in the locker room for the first time in 1991 in San Antonio, he seemed like a towering evangelist. The story below originally appeared in Sports Spectrum Magazine *in 1991. We've included Robinson's story here because he has some incredible things to say about his relationship with Christ. Keep in mind, though, that he was not speaking at a church service on Sunday morning. He was standing in the middle of the Spurs locker room as his teammates and some surprised members of the media looked on.*

The scene is San Antonio, Texas. Home to the Alamo, a beautiful river walk and David Maurice Robinson, the 7-foot-1-inch center for the San Antonio Spurs.

Robinson began playing here in 1989 and, since that time, the Hemisphere Arena in San Antonio has unofficially become known as "Mr. Robinson's Neighborhood."

On this particular night, however, the neighborhood is not happy. Houston's Sleepy Floyd, who was shooting less than 50 percent from the floor with .7 seconds left in this game with the Spurs, throws in a miraculous shot from half court to tie the game at 97-97 and send the contest into overtime. Just moments before the shot, most of Robinson's neighborhood had started for the exits, thinking that the game was well in tow. Now, however, most of the stunned crowd found themselves wandering incredulously back to their seats and looking on in disbelief as the Spurs lose 112-110 in double OT.

Back in the locker room after the game, Robinson, his teammates and the Spurs coaching staff are trying to figure out how Floyd was able to get his shot off in the first place. As it turned out, Robinson and his teammates had gotten somewhat turned around on the play, leaving Floyd, who is not known for his three-point prowess, free to shoot the game-tying three-pointer.

It is apparent that Robinson is disgusted with both himself and his teammates but, in a way that is hard to explain, he also appears almost matter-of-fact about this particular loss that drops the Spurs' early-season record to 16-14.

"We just can't let this turn into a slide," he tells several reporters who have gathered after the game. "We should have won tonight."

As he talks, you get the feeling that there is something different about David Robinson aside from the fact that he scored 1,320 on his SAT exam and has a mathematics degree from the United States Naval Academy. A casual conversation with Robinson leaves you with the feeling that this is a young man who could have been successful in any profession that he wanted to go into. A heart surgeon, perhaps. Or maybe a federal prosecutor, with his 7 feet 1 inch frame peering down over a powerful drug czar in a packed courtroom.

Whatever his career might have been, all of San Antonio seems to be glad that Robinson chose basketball.

"David is to San Antonio what Michael Jordan is to Chicago or Larry Bird is to the Celtics," said Spurs coach Larry Brown. "He's a pretty special kid, not just on the court, where he does so much, but off the court as well. He's one of the guys we look to for leadership on this team. He's been through some changes over the past year and all of them, it seems, have helped him to become a better player. He just keeps getting better."

One of the most important changes in Robinson's life came last June after a visit with an Austin minister.

"In June, a minister from Austin came down and talked to me," Robinson said. "He basically pointed at me and told me that I wasn't living a Christian life and that I needed to take my Christian life very seriously. It really pointed at a place in my heart because, in 1986, I prayed with an evangelist on the plane coming back from Amsterdam after the world championships (U.S. Olympic Games). In fact, it was me and Kenny Smith (now with Houston). We prayed to accept Jesus Christ into our hearts but we didn't really know what it entailed, we didn't really make the commitment, we really didn't make that change. But I knew that I should have been reading the Bible and trying to learn more about the Lord and I did here and there but I didn't really seek it out. And, this summer, I think that's why it struck such a cord in my heart when that minister from Austin told me that I wasn't really doing the job of a Christian and being in the Kingdom. June 8 was the time that I vowed to commit my life to the Lord and, when I did that, the Lord really blessed me in a great way. He opened up all my senses and made me turn all my energies into the Word."

For Robinson, a man of many interests, this was unusual. He is an extremely rare individual in that, unlike a lot of his NBA friends and most of the general population, Robinson likes to engage in many endeavors and endeavors to do them all well. Besides being an outstanding basketball player, he is also somewhat of a classical pianist, settling behind the keyboards studying Mozart almost as quickly as he goes to the backboards against Karl Malone. While also an avid golfer, Robinson has said that if he wasn't playing professional basketball, he would be like to be wearing a major league baseball uniform. Such is the diverse neighborhood of Mr. Robinson. Everything seems to interest him and, even in casual conversation, it is easy to see that he has a voracious appetite for knowledge and an unusually intense desire to learn about new things.

While Robinson still prides himself in being well-rounded, it is also apparent that he is more focused now as there is a single-mindedness about him these days that might have been missing prior to June 8, 1991.

"I had been so spread out," Robinson said. "I was just into everything with music and basketball and playing golf and doing all kinds of different things, trying to get really good at different things. But I just dropped everything and got into the Word. Soon, I got into fellowship with other believers and began praying all the time. Suddenly, in about two months, God really blessed me with a lot of knowledge and a lot of His wisdom and gave me a message that, by September, I had to be strong. And I didn't understand why at first. But I started to understand when September began to come around and my team started to come back.

"In the summer, it was easy to be immersed in the Word and immersed with just Christian friends and really build up spiritually. But when you start playing ball again and start getting around other guys with a different lifestyle, you really have to be strong and you have to know what you want and have your habits already formed and I was starting to understand why that was so important to me. Since I came back in here, I have been on fire and have been trying to get these guys to wake up and to understand that God is really tapping them on the shoulder and that it is time to get right with God. And it has been beautiful because God has really given me so much with basketball."

While at the Naval Academy in Annapolis, Robinson earned the nickname "The Admiral" because of the way he always seemed to take charge of his fellow midshipmen and lead them to victory on the basketball court. When you thought of college basketball in the mid-1980s, Robinson was usually in a class by himself. But life in the NBA is not as easy as it is the college ranks. Leaders abound here and it is no secret that many of college basketball's brightest stars never make good on what once seemed like a blank check in the NBA.

Robinson, however, is one of the few players who has captured not only stardom but also a tremendous amount of respect from his teammates during his three short seasons with the Spurs. There is no question who the Spurs look to when the game is on the line and few can control the tempo of a game the way Robinson does with his assortment of reverse slams and jams.

But while Robinson has been leading the team in almost every category imaginable for the last three seasons, it was only last summer when he realized that God wanted him to do more than just score 30 points a game.

"During the 1990-91 season, Coach (Larry) Brown kept telling me 'You're not being a leader, you're not being a leader' and I didn't really understand what he was talking about," Robinson said. "I'd say 'Hey, what are you talking about? I'm getting 30 points a game, 16 rebounds a game. Five blocked shots. I mean, what do you want? What's being a leader, anyway?' And I didn't understand. But when I started studying God's Word, God started showing me what being a leader is about and the one verse that just changed my whole walk was Joshua 1:5-8.

"The Lord was talking to Joshua after Moses had died and Joshua was a little shaky about taking over because Moses was such a great man. But what God was telling Joshua was 'Hey, Moses is dead.' It was the same thing that God was telling me. The verse says that 'No man will be able to stand against you all the days of your life. As I was with Moses, so I will be with you.' And it really just seemed like the Lord was telling this to me: 'Moses was a great man. Joshua was a great man. Job was a great man and all these people were great men but they are dead and it is time for you to rise up and be a leader.' Not only in my Christian walk but here with this team and in this league and as an athlete in this profession.

"God said 'No man will be able to stand up against you. Don't back down from anyone. As I was with Moses, so I will be with you' and that was powerful to me. And He said 'I will never leave you nor forsake you so be very strong and courageous for you will lead these people to inherit the land that I promised to give to their forefathers. Do not let this book depart from your mouth. Meditate on it day and night so that you will be careful to do everything in it and then you will be prosperous and successful.'"

Robinson is on a post-game roll now. Except for a few coaches, a handful of writers from the local media and the equipment boys, the locker room has all but cleared out.

Robinson, however, remains focused in the book of Joshua. He will be the first to tell you that he doesn't consider himself to have a very long attention span. Yet, at this particular point in time, he is as intense as a Billy Sunday or a Billy Graham.

"When the Lord tells you things like 'Don't be terrified. Don't be discouraged' those are powerful things," Robinson said. "But it's hard not to get discouraged. When David was fighting Goliath, the whole Israeli army was looking at this nine-foot man and they were terrified. Nobody wanted to face him. But then along comes David and he's not going by what he sees, he's going by what he knows to be true. He sees this great giant and says, in effect, 'Who is this? Who is this clown standing against the armies of the Lord? Does he understand that he is not just fighting me, he's fighting the Lord?' And everybody else is terrified and I look at this team and I see that these guys don't really understand what I'm talking about yet, and it's a chance to get frustrated because people's lives don't change overnight. It takes them time to really understand and time to see it working in your life. People are not going to change to something that they don't see is powerful and that it really works. So I just try to be a light for them and not get discouraged. It's like God is saying 'I've got it all worked out. Don't be discouraged. You may not be able to see exactly what I'm doing but I'm doing it. I'm working in their hearts and their minds and they are going to see that I am God.' That is something you see throughout the Bible."

Robinson went on to relate a story about Moses.

"When Moses found out that he was a Hebrew, he told himself that he was going to deliver his people," Robinson said. "But when he tries it his own way, he kills one Egyptian at a time. And it got frustrating for him and then they chased him out of town. Then it took 40 years for the Lord to pound that pompous pride out of him. But later it says that

Moses was the most humble man on earth. That's a powerful statement.

"When God first came to Moses and told him that he was going to lead his people out of Egypt, Moses turned to him and said, 'Why me? I'm 80 years old and I don't have the ability to do this.' That's how the Lord wants you when he wants to work with you. He doesn't want you all pompous and arrogant. It really taught me a lot about my role here. I can't hold these guys's hands. All I can do is plant that seed and just hope that I set a good example.

"I've just been plugging away and have been real encouraged and have just had a joy every day about it. I think that, in time, they are going to see that, just because I'm a fanatic for God, it doesn't mean I'm soft on the court. I can come out here and bust up Patrick (Ewing) or Hakeem (Olajuwon) and I can hit somebody just as hard as someone else can. And that is just something that I hope sinks in. Christianity is a powerful lifestyle. One of the most powerful men ever was Jesus. He never backed down from anybody and I think that's how the Lord wants you to live your life. You've got to get into people's faces and challenge them with God's standards. You have to tell people that these are God's standards and that He is not going to make it any easier for anybody."

Robinson was also quick to note that, while society's standards have become increasingly lax over the years, God's standards never change.

"You have to say 'This is the standard, and if you can't live up to it, than you have to suffer the consequences,'" Robinson said. "As a Christian, you just have to make people realize that you are not going to accept anything less than God's standard."

It is not long after that that Robinson excuses himself and begins to gather up his gear. Before he goes, however, he has one final thing to say.

"We're all called to be winners," he said. "It's exciting to be a Christian and to be going about the Lord's work and I'm thankful for the opportunities He has given me here."

The Spurs may have let one slip away in overtime on this rainy January night in San Antonio but, to David Maurice Robinson, basketball is a game that ultimately pales in comparison with God's vast game of life.

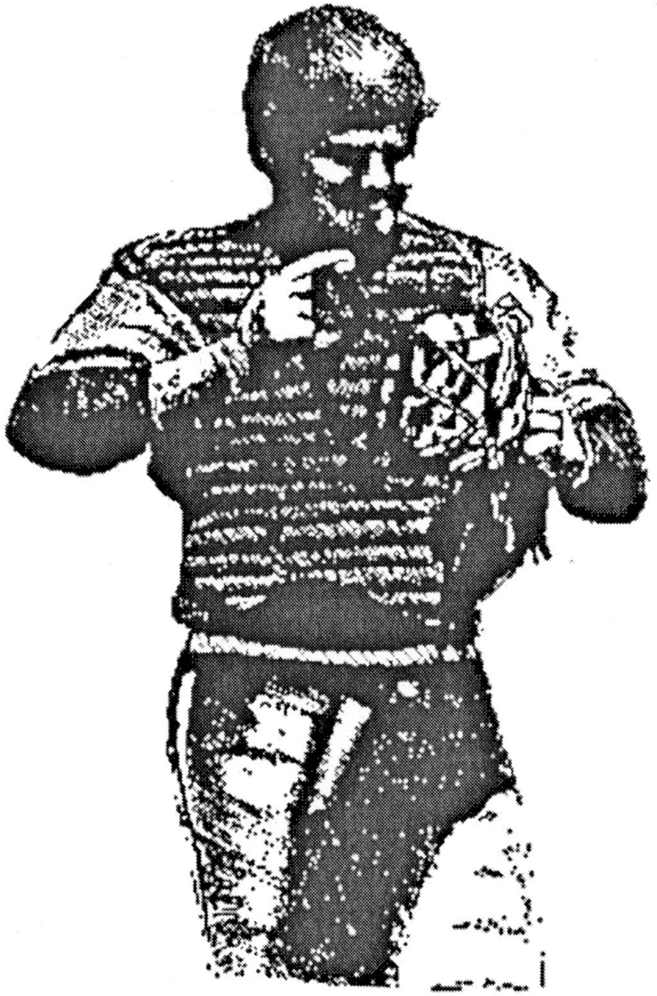

Jim Sundberg

Man Behind the Mask

Jim Sundberg has been a good friend for many years. During the 1990s, Sunny was a regular at the Athletes in Action Drug-Free Assemblies that we did at various schools in the Dallas-Fort Worth area. The athletes would play basketball, tug-of-war and compete in other activities with the students and then Jim or one of the other athletes would tell them how important it is to stay drug free. Below is an old Athletes In Action newsletter that we put together in the early 1990s that says all the things that we really wanted to say in those public school assemblies.

The year was 1977 and a young Jim Sundberg was gradually establishing himself as one of the top catchers in the American League. Along with New York's Thurman Munson and Boston's Carlton Fisk, the 26-year-old backstop from Galesburg, Illinois was quickly earning respect around the American League for his ability to gun down opposing base runners. In 1977, he had already won his second Gold Glove Award, edging out Munson and Fisk as the American

League's top defensive catcher. He was also becoming a threat offensively.

Nineteen-seventy-seven turned out to be one of Jim's best years at the plate as he hit .291 and drove in 65 runs for the Texas Rangers that year. Since being drafted by the Rangers in June of 1972 and joining the parent club in 1974, 1977 was without question the most memorable year of Jim Sundberg's life.

What made it memorable, however, was not so much the success that he found against opposing pitchers but, rather, the victory he claimed after a little known pitcher from Atlanta was dealt to the Rangers the previous year.

"Adrian Devine had just been acquired by the Rangers from Atlanta," Sundberg said. "He had given me a book by Hal Lindsey called *The Late, Great Planet Earth*. I read that book and I began thinking about why we're here on earth and what our purpose is. Adrian and I began to talk some more and he began to share the Gospel of Jesus Christ with me. In June of 1977, I accepted Christ as my personal Savior in my hotel room in Toronto."

It was in that hotel room that Jim Sundberg turned his life over to God, much like Christ was talking about in John 3:3 when he told Nicodemus, "I tell you the truth, unless a man is born again, he cannot see the Kingdom of God." By this simple act of faith, Jim Sundberg assured and secured himself a place in God's Hall of Fame.

"I was raised in the church and I thought I was a pretty good person," he said, "but I never had an assurance of salvation. But, that night, I began to get a greater sense of who God was and, by accepting Christ's finished work on the cross and confessing my sins before him, I could know for sure that I would go to heaven."

Some eight years after Jim accepted Christ as his Savior in that hotel room in Toronto, he got some big hits and made some key plays to help his new team, the Kansas City Royals, defeat the St. Louis Cardinals and win the 1985 World Series.

But, while Jim will be the first to tell you that a World Series ring was the highlight of his baseball career, he'll also be quick to add that, compared to the Kingdom of God, the luster of a World Series ring quickly pales in comparison.

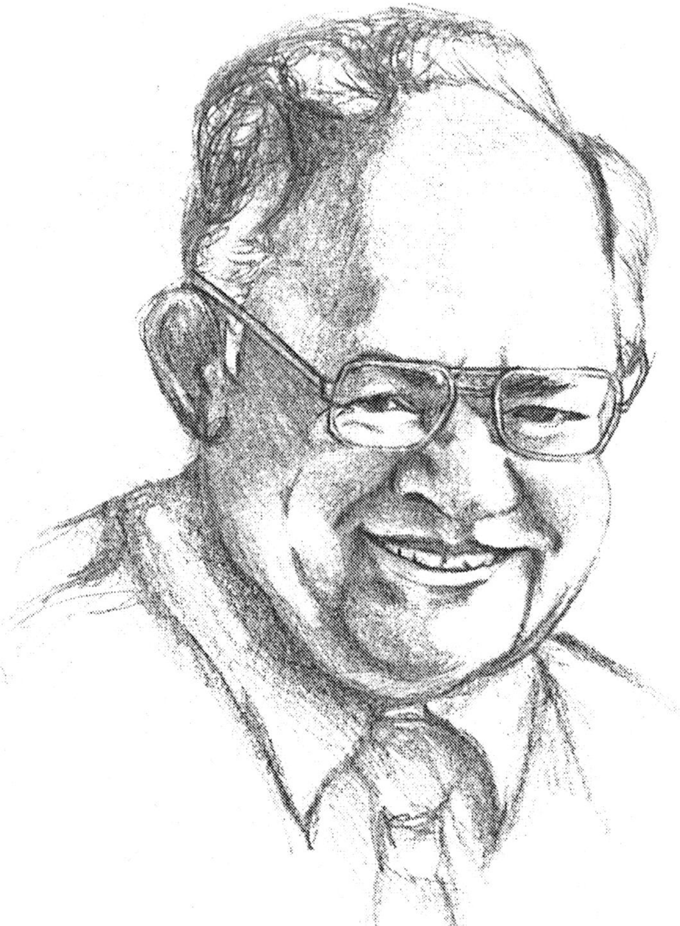

Dave Thomas

"You're Fired!"

It's no fun getting fired from a job. But as Dave Thomas points out during this interview, sometimes God can turn a bad break into a big blessing. It was fun to visit with Dave on the telephone back in 1994 and it's sad to think that he's not with us anymore. Talking to Dave Thomas on the phone was like talking to a neighbor over the back fence. He was a multi-millionaire and a star in his own right. Yet, when we interviewed him that day, he kept referring to himself as "just a guy who sells hamburgers."

Dave Thomas, Senior Chairman and Founder of Wendy's International, remembers the incident like it happened yesterday.

"I had just been fired from my second job in about a month and, when my dad found out, he got so mad I thought the veins in his neck would burst," Thomas wrote in his autobiography, *Dave's Way*. "He slammed his fist on the kitchen table and screamed 'You'll never keep a job! I'll be supporting you for the rest of your life!'"

At the time, a young Thomas was only 12 years old and living in Knoxville, Tenn. A month earlier he had been delivering groceries for a local grocery store. When the owner of the store told Dave that he was closing the store for two weeks because he was going on vacation, Thomas was delighted. Two weeks at the local swimming pool with his friends suited Dave just fine!

But when the owner came back after only one week and called him back in to work, Thomas told him that, since he thought he was going to be off, he had already made other plans for the week. The next day, Dave passed the grocery store and saw a 'Help Wanted' sign in the window. He knew then that he had been fired.

"I can still see the 'Help Wanted' sign in the window of that grocery store," he wrote in his autobiography *Dave's Way*. "It's sort of a symbol of what I learned from that experience. I learned that when you take a job, you'd better be ready to show up when it suits your boss, not just when it suits you."

Three weeks later, while working at Walgreen's Drug Store in Knoxville, Dave was fired from another job when the owner found out that the 12-year-old Thomas was not the 16-year-old boy he said he was.

Losing that second job was bad enough; not getting any sympathy at home was even worse.

"I expected my dad to understand," Dave said, recalling the incident in a telephone interview from his home in Fort Lauderdale, Florida. "But when he didn't and then told me that I would never be able to hold a job, that really lit a fire under me. I was determined to never lose another job the rest of my life and, fortunately, I didn't."

Thomas may not have realized it at the time, but that day proved to be a turning point in his life. Since that day, he became not only an outstanding employee, but he has also created thousands of jobs around the world for employees of his Wendy's restaurants.

At his next job, the Regas Restaurant in Knoxville, Thomas put in 12 to 14 hour days, preparing food, busing tables and doing whatever else needed to be done. After a few months, Thomas finally confessed to his employer that he was only 12 and not 16.

But because of his determination and because he had become such a valuable employee, the owners, Frank and George Regas, decided to keep him around.

Thomas worked there four more months before his adoptive father decided to move the family again, this time back to Indiana. But before he left, the owners wanted to make one thing clear - if Dave ever needed a job, he would certainly be welcome back at the Regas Restaurant.

"It was tough moving around so much," Thomas said. "Everybody has cliques. They've always been here and they always will be here. Moving around so much, I always seemed to be the outsider. Plus, I also had three stepsisters and it seemed like I was always the outsider at home as well. I would always get the last of everything - the last bed, the last pillow, the last coat. Whatever it was, I always got whatever was left over. Maybe that's why I enjoyed working at the restaurant so much. There, I felt like I fit in and belonged. In a sense, the restaurant was my family because there I felt accepted."

It was at about that time that Thomas found out he was adopted.

"I didn't find out that I was adopted until I was 13," he said. "And, when I found that out, I got mad. I was just mad at everybody. I was mad at my real mom and dad for abandoning me. I was mad at my adoptive mom and dad for not telling me. I was just mad at everybody. Everybody, that is, except for my grandmother. Other than the people at the restaurants I worked in, she was the only person who ever seemed to show any interest in me while I was growing up."

Her name was Minnie Sinclair and, from the time Thomas was between the ages of 7 and 13 years old, she was a steady influence in his life.

"She would always take me to the dime store on Saturdays," Thomas said. "She never made much money, but she always seemed to have money. She raised her own vegetables and she worked at a local restaurant, cooking and washing dishes. She was a hard worker and always stressed quality. When we didn't go to the dime store, we would sell vegetables out by a roadside stand by her house. Of all the people I've met during my life, I would have to say that Minnie Sinclair is my all-time hero. She always stood for honesty, integrity and telling the truth. She had a major impact on my life."

It was also through Minnie Sinclair that Dave realized how he could know for sure where he would spend eternity. Values were fine, but without Christ they meant very little.

"My grandmother talked to me a lot about heaven and hell and how important it was to have a relationship with Jesus," he said. "She was a strong Baptist and talked a lot about how a person could know for sure whether he would go to heaven or hell and that it was up to each of us to decide where we were going to spend eternity."

At the age of 15, Dave dropped out of school after the 10th grade. He didn't really want to leave school but, after working 50 hours a week part-time and trying to study too, he found that he just couldn't do it any more.

"Dropping out of school was a big mistake," he said. "I should have never dropped out of high school but, when I look back on it, I really didn't have a lot of choice. I was working

Real American Heroes

50 hours a week at the restaurant part-time and I was tired of moving every few months with my family. Plus, the people at the restaurant where I was working had sort of become my family and I didn't want to leave them. Fortunately, things worked out for me but that was a long time ago. I certainly don't recommend that route for anybody today."

Forty-six years later, on Feb. 20, 1993, Thomas took and passed his G.E.D. test and earned the equivalent of a high school diploma. By that time, Thomas had become a multimillionaire through his Wendy's restaurant chain. But part of standing for quality means finishing what you start, even if it means going back and picking up where you left off 46 years ago.

"Obviously, I felt like getting my high school diploma was important or I wouldn't have gone back after all those years," he said. "Education is just so important these days.

"Whatever you do, you have to prepare for it. If you want to be a writer, you have to go to journalism school and learn how to be a writer. If you're going to be a teacher, you have to go to school to learn how to be a good teacher. It's the same way in the restaurant business. If you like restaurants and would like to own your own restaurant some day, you have to prepare for it and that means getting a good education as well as putting in long hours working in a restaurant so you can know the business inside out."

In 1950, Thomas joined the army and it was there that a painful root canal surgery proved to be a great blessing for him. Instead of staying in bed feeling sorry for himself after having dental surgery, Thomas went down to the kitchen to see if he could help out. For a few weeks he cleared tables, swept up and helped out the cooks. He did such a good job that it wasn't long before he was asked if he wanted to go to Cook and Baker's School. For a man who had spent years wanting to be in the restaurant business, it was an easy question.

Although he will be the first to tell you that he's never been much of a baker, the school taught Thomas a lot about the big picture of the restaurant business.

"If you don't have anything to do, time passes so slowly and that was the situation I was in when I was in the army when I had that root canal done," Thomas said. "I could have stayed in bed for two weeks after I had that done. I had a note from my dentist. But I really felt that I needed to be up doing something so I went down to the kitchen to help out and the next thing I knew I was in baker's school. I didn't like that very much, the baking end of it, but I did learn a lot and that experience taught me to always volunteer for things and always take the initiative. I wouldn't want to do it over again, but my overall experience in the army taught me a great deal."

By the late 1950s, Thomas was a civilian again, working for the Hobby Ranch House Restaurant chain in the Mid-West and hooking up with a famous colonel, although this one was not in the military.

Few knew who Colonel Harland Sanders was at that time but now he is known far and wide as the founder of Kentucky Fried Chicken. His secret recipe for fried chicken was to put both Thomas and the Colonel on the restaurant map to stay.

Sanders approached the Hobby Ranch House with his idea for chicken and the restaurant started carrying it. Later, when Thomas took over four of Hobby Ranch House's failing restaurants in Columbus, Ohio, he changed the name of the restaurants so that customers would see an emphasis on chicken.

The Hobby Ranch House restaurants in Columbus suddenly became "Colonel Sanders Kentucky Fried Chicken Take-Home." A little bit longer than the "KFC" signs that one sees on highway billboards today but, never the less, Kentucky Fried Chicken and a whole new fast food or, as Dave would say "quick-serve," industry was born.

In 1968, at the age of 35, Thomas sold all of his shares of KFC stock. The sale made him a millionaire and, the following year, he opened up his first Wendy's restaurant in Columbus, Ohio.

"I had always wanted to have my own restaurant and maybe envisioned having two or three more around town, but I never imagined it getting as big as it did," Thomas said.

If there is one thing that Thomas knows, it is how to make a good hamburger. Evidently, a lot of people think he makes a pretty good one.

Since that first Wendy's opened on Nov. 15, 1969 in Columbus, Thomas has opened almost 4,000 other Wendy's restaurants around the world. Not only can you get one of Dave's specialty burgers almost anywhere in the United States, you can also get one in Turkey, West Germany, Indonesia, Greece and Guatemala.

All this success, however, hasn't gone to Dave's head. Whenever someone spots him in a crowd and says to him "Aren't you somebody famous?" his typical response is "I'm just a guy who makes hamburgers." And then it dawns on the person that this is "Wendy's dad."

His business has made him a multi-millionaire, yet he is still as humble as he was when he was working those 14-hour shifts as a young boy.

"Money makes a lot of people crazy," Thomas said. "They don't know how to handle it. They take drugs, they buy a lot of stuff they don't need or it causes them to lose sight of who they are. Their possessions control them instead of the other way around. I think that when you have a business that is blessed, you have an obligation to give something back and that's what I try to do."

Thomas is a generous contributor to various organizations such as the Dr. Arthur James Cancer Research Hospital at Ohio State University, the Children's Home Society in Florida and the St. Jude Children's Research Hospital.

[The first] President Bush also named Thomas to be the national spokesman for the "Adoption Works...For Everyone" campaign and Thomas travels around the country talking to people about the importance of adoption and how it works.

"Because of adoption, I got a chance," he said. "That's what everybody deserves and that's all that anybody can ask for."

Not only did Dave Thomas get the chance, he made the most of it. Many times over.

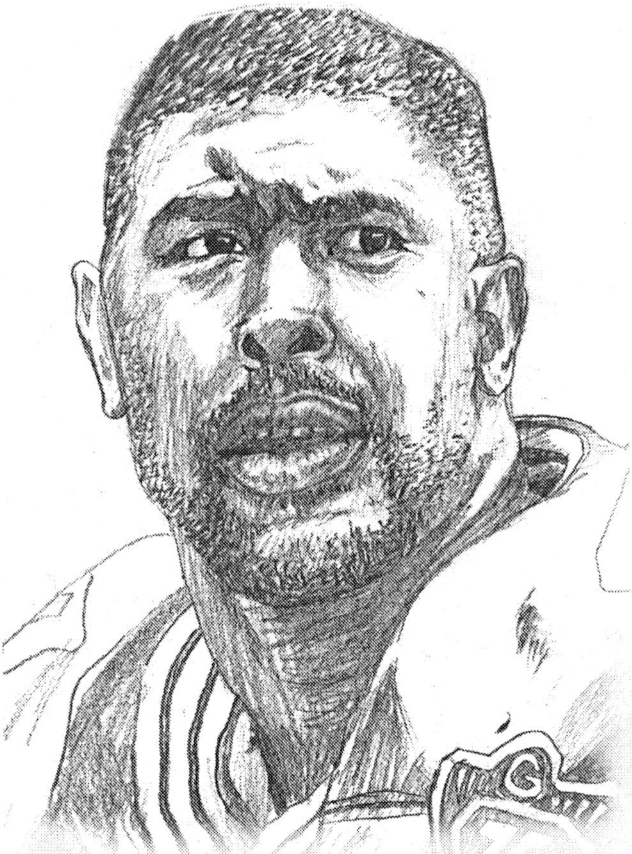

Reggie White

Minister of Defense

Reggie White is a man who is not afraid to speak his mind. When we caught up with him in October of 1992 in Philadelphia for this story for the 1993 Super Bowl Edition of Sports Spectrum Magazine, he was unapologetic in his stand for Christ. But he also made it clear that he can't do alone. Tragically, the Lord called Reggie White home on December 26, 2004, just seven days after his 43rd birthday. An autopsy revealed that White likely died of an uncommon respiratory disease known as sarcoidosis, which may have been exacerbated by sleep apnea.

The signs displayed in Veterans Stadium on this cold, windy day in Philadelphia seemed to say it all.

Across the upper deck at about the 50-yard line, a huge banner read, "1-800-WAKE-UP." Another placard, prominently displayed in one of the end zones, proclaimed encouragingly, "Don't Fret! You're at the Vet!"

But if the Eagles themselves weren't fretting, it was evident that a wake-up call wouldn't be a bad idea.

After embarrassing the Dallas Cowboys 31-7 at Veterans Stadium earlier in the month, the Eagles had dropped two straight games and had seen their previously unblemished record fall to 4-2.

Even worse, the Eagle offense, a potent force that had generated more than 30 points against Phoenix, Denver and Dallas earlier in the season, had scored a total of 29 points in its last two games against the Chiefs and Redskins. The 24-17 loss at Kansas City's Arrowhead Stadium and the 16-12 loss at Washington had sent Eagle fans home shaking their heads. Now, with the 1-6 Cardinals in town and the season almost half gone, it was time to get back into the win column.

Philadelphia struck first, scoring with 8:24 left in the first half on a 40-yard pass play to wide receiver Calvin Williams and the Eagles appeared to be on their way to an easy victory over the Cards.

But after that TD, the Eagle offense began to sputter, then stall, then stop completely. Final score: Philadelphia 7, Phoenix 3.

One local pundit joked that the Philadelphia Flyers could outscore the Eagles. Another scribe dryly added that he hadn't been this excited since he saw the movie *Ishtar*.

They had a point. It was not a spectacular win. In fact, had it not been for Reggie White and the rest of the Eagles' defensive unit, the Cardinals probably would have flown back west with a W.

"We're going to have to stop counting on Reggie to keep saving games for us," said Eagles cornerback Eric Allen. "He kept us in the ballgame and came through with some big plays when we needed them most."

One of those times came late in the first half as the Eagles held on to a slim 7-0 lead. The Cardinals were driving and had the ball at the Eagle 3-yard line. Because of two Philadelphia penalties, Arizona got seven shots at pay dirt from three yards out or less. The Eagle defense, however, just said "No."

"We've had goal-line stands before, but nothing like that," White marveled after the game. "The two penalties down there made the situation even tougher for us, but fortunately, we were able to keep them from scoring."

The game came down to one play - a screen pass over the middle to Cardinal running back Larry Centers. Only moments before, White had batted down a Tim Rosenbach pass to force a fourth-and-11 situation.

Now, with just over two minutes remaining in the game and the ball at the Eagle 22, the Cardinals were just one touchdown away from their second win of the season.

White, however, charged through the line and nearly sacked Rosenbach, who got the ball off hurriedly but it fell incomplete. The Eagles took over and held on for the victory. Reggie had delivered his wake-up call.

"You try to keep two guys on him because you just can't handle him man-to-man," said Phoenix head coach Joe Bugel. "Another second or two and we might have gotten that play off. And we would have, too, had it not been for Reggie. Had we gotten that first down, we might have been able to pull that game out."

Life as well as football is often a game of inches and big plays in which leaders lead by example. White will be the first to tell you that to be a leader in the game of football you also have to be a leader in the game of life.

White has earned great respect in the NFL, but it's nothing new. The people who knew him when he was in college at Tennessee feel the same way.

"Basically, Reggie is the same today as he was when he was playing football for the University of Tennessee," says 33-year-old Avery Huff, who played on two UT football teams with White. Whatever White does, Huff said, he always goes after it with gusto.

"He always gives 100 percent," Huff said, "whether it's his relationship with God or his talent in football or his relationship with his family. People see that he is serious about what he does and about his relationship with the Lord, and I think that's why both Christians and non-Christians respect him so much."

Perhaps another reason is that White does not criticize those who don't know Christ as their Savior. Instead, White says he tries to set an example and be the kind of person that God has called him to be.

"The thing I'm learning about living for Jesus is that it's not what you say but how you live," White says. "You can talk about Jesus all you want to, but if you aren't living the life that God has called you to live, nobody's going to respect you and they aren't going to respect the God you are serving."

White has observed that many players in the NFL are turning to Islam and other religions simply because they see more commitment in those who serve other gods.

"The difference between Christians and Muslims is that Muslims are often more faithful to their god than we are to ours," White said. "A lot of people don't want to be Christians because they don't see any commitment. I heard of a situation where one of the greatest basketball players who ever played the game became a Muslim because he saw more commitment in the Muslim faith than he saw in the Christian faith. He also saw more hypocrites in the Christian faith. And that's what has happened to not only a large number of prominent athletes but also a lot of people in general because they don't see a commitment in the Christian faith. So, as a result, they go and look for other things that they feel are real."

Which brings up a good point. How do we know that God *is* real or that Christ *is* who He said He is?

"The thing is, is that *I* know," White explains. "Some people just don't want to know. You look at atheists. They know there's a God. They know if there wasn't, they wouldn't be fighting so hard to disprove that there is no God. You look at Madalyn Murray O'Hair, a woman who says she doesn't believe in God and yet she is a woman who has spent her whole life trying to get God out of the schools. I know God is real. I know personally He's real and a lot of other people know God is real and, as I say, people either don't know or they don't want to believe. The Bible says that a natural man does not understand the things of the Spirit. That's the only way you can really explain it."

White says that it is also difficult to explain to some people why just being a "good" person and believing in God is not good enough.

"A lot of people just can't understand why they need a relationship with Christ," White said. "I'll try to tell them about Jesus and they'll say, 'Well, I believe in God.' But I tell people that there is a difference between 'belief' and having faith in God. There are a lot of people who believe in God but who are going to hell. And the Bible says that even demons believe in the truth. They believe in God and yet they don't have a personal relationship with Jesus. What it boils down to is having a personal relationship with Christ."

Still, Reggie said he can understand why some people are turned off by Christianity.

"In a lot of ways, you really can't blame people for rejecting the Gospel, because the church as a whole is not showing the example that it needs to in order to win people to Jesus and keep them there," White said. "Sometimes, I think the church has hurt more people concerning the Kingdom of

God than it has helped. A lot of people have this Pharisee-type of attitude that says, 'Hey, if you aren't living this way or that way, you're going to hell.' The thing that is so interesting in the Scriptures is that Jesus told Peter that if he truly loved Him, Peter would feed his sheep (see John 21:15-20)."

Many people think that the kind of life Christ wants a person to live will make a person seem too soft. That, White said, is simply not true.

"Actually, it makes you more of a man," he said. "It takes a man to serve Christ because of all the trouble we have to go through because we are Christians. The devil is going to bring as much difficulty on you as he can. In I Peter 4:12 it says, 'Don't fear when darkness and tribulation come about.' We have to go through stuff. We have to hurt. But Jesus said rejoice in that hurt.

"Think about the apostles. They were beaten and died very violent deaths. There were times when, after they were beaten, they went out rejoicing because they felt privileged to be beaten like Jesus was beaten. When Paul and Silas were in prison, they were singing hymns. I'm sure they were hurting, because the Scriptures say that their backs were beaten. But they found it a privilege to go through the same things that Jesus went through.

"If you look at our country, we don't really have much to complain about. You look at other countries, and people are having it hard, but the only thing they have to trust in is Jesus.

"The greatest gift in life," White said, "may be the one that people never accept. People are missing out on the greatest gift God has ever given them when they don't accept Christ. Everybody is going to have to give an account for it. The great men and the great women are going to have to stand before God right alongside the poor men and the poor women."

By that time, even the Minister of Defense would admit that it's far too late for a wake-up call.

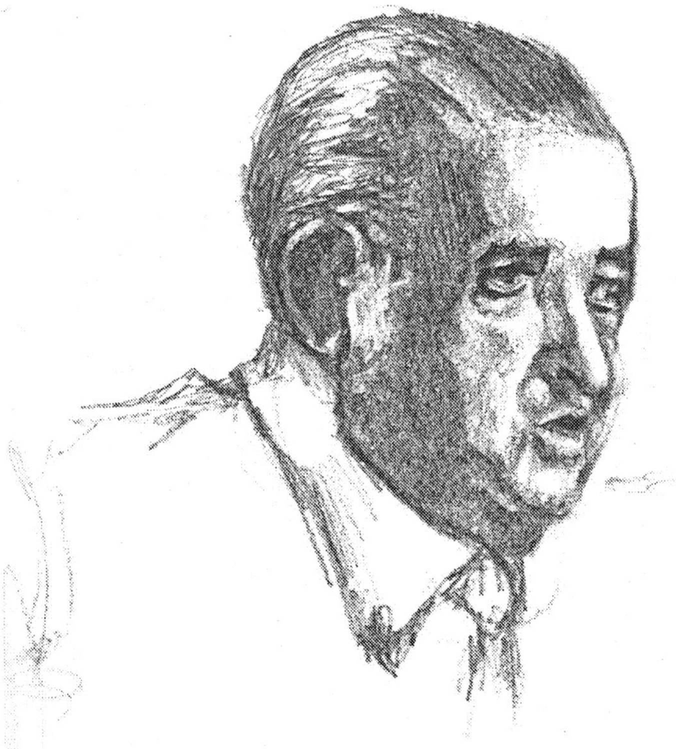

Gordon Wood

Winning Values, Winning Ways

If you ask any Texas football coach at any level who Gordon Wood was, they wouldn't have any problem telling you. Wood set the standard for high school coaches in both wins and integrity. He had been so successful and we had heard so much about him that we wanted to go out to Brownwood and see for ourselves what made him tick. Graciously, he invited us into his home and we talked X's, O's and about the secrets behind a successful high school football program. It was a strange interview, however, in that we were talking to one of the greatest high school football coaches in history and yet we were doing it while watching the NCAA college basketball tournament. The story below was written shortly after we visited with him in the early 1990s.

He has won more football games than anyone in the history of Texas high school football. In 43 seasons as a head football coach (26 at Brownwood High School), he compiled an incredible 405-88-12 record before retiring at the end of the 1985 season. He is respected throughout the country as perhaps the greatest high school football coach of all-time.

So, naturally, on this warm, March day in Brownwood, Gordon Wood, the winningest high school football coach in the state of Texas is ... *watching basketball?*

"I think he loves this NCAA basketball tournament as much as he does football," said Wood's better-half Katharine, who has been his wife for more than 50 years.

"All of the four teams that I predicted would be in the Final Four are still in the hunt," Wood interjects. "Duke should win this game here."

Duke goes on to win its game and Wood, the football genius-turned-basketball prognosticator, has yet another one of his picks headed for the Final Four.

Between basketball playoff games, Wood talks football but, mostly, he talks about the players and teams who helped him win more than 400 games.

"It's really pretty amazing when you think about it," he said. "There were a lot of years when we didn't have a real big team or didn't have a lot of speed but yet managed to win a state championship. Then, we've had other years where we've had better teams, but didn't even win the district. Most people don't realize what a small difference there is between winning and losing. Plus, a lot of the success you have in football has to do with how you feel mentally. If you think you have a chance to beat a team in a game where you are a huge underdog, than you can probably beat them, especially if the other team is overconfident."

Such was the case in Wood's first season at Brownwood High in 1960. Brownwood was picked sixth that season and was a four-touchdown underdog against San Angelo. Wood's team rolled to a 34-6 decision that day and, from there, Brownwood went on to win the first of its seven state championships.

"They were picked to just run over us," Wood said, smiling as he thinks back on it now. "But our boys felt like we had a chance to win and, when you think you've got a chance, sometimes that's all you need."

When pressed to explain his success, Wood is quick to point to the character of his teams and his coaching staff. But, beyond that, a great deal of his success on the football field has lied in the intangibles.

"There were several years when we won the state championship but didn't have all that much talent," he said. "When we won the state championship at Stamford in 1955, I had no idea before the season started that we would win it. At one of the district meetings, a coach from another team had suggested that Stamford was going to win the state championship that year. Well, it got into the newspaper and it wasn't long before the whole town started buzzing about how we were going to win a state championship in football. I was so mad that I was fit to be tied. I knew we weren't going to win a state championship.

"Yet, the players on our team kept talking about it and, in an impromptu moment, I gathered all my coaches together and told them that every time a player comes up to you and asks you if you think that there is a chance that we can win the state championship, you tell them that, if we work hard, you don't see any reason why we can't. As it turned out, we had an incredible season that year and we won a state championship. Oddly enough, I've had better teams than that Stamford team that didn't win a state championship. The thing about it, though, was that that team had as much character as any team that I've ever coached."

One of those players on that 1955 state championship team was U.S. Congressman Charles Stenholm. The congressman and his high school football coach keep in touch to this day, remaining the best of friends.

"Out of about 36 boys that I had on that team, I think there were about 34 of them that went on to graduate from college," Wood said. "It was just an incredible team that felt like it could win and usually did."

But, to Wood, winning wasn't the only thing that mattered.

"Winning is important, but kids are in school to get an education," he said. "Some coaches lose sight of that and it winds up hurting kids."

As Wood headed into his second full season at Rule High School in 1941, he almost lost sight of that himself.

"We had had a good team in 1940 and I was looking forward to another good year in 1941," Wood said. "One day, one of my players comes up to me and tells me that three of my players are going to flunk out of school. I immediately went up to the superintendent's office and told him that if he didn't make sure that those kids passed, I was going to resign. He told me he would see what he could do. The next day, the superintendent told me that he had talked to the teachers and that all three boys would pass.

"Later that day, I saw my quarterback and he asked me if the three were going to pass. I told him that I thought that they would pass. My quarterback told me that one of the players in question had told a teacher 'If you don't think enough of my football to pass me, you don't think enough of it.' When I heard that, I turned right around and went back into the superintendent's office. I told him that we were about to ruin three kids and that, if he did pass them, I was going to resign."

Real American Heroes

The students didn't pass and Wood stayed.

"I learned a valuable lesson from that experience," he said. "That was the last time that I ever talked to a teacher, a principal or a superintendent about a kid's grade. After that, I just stayed out of it."

But "staying out of it" didn't mean that Wood didn't care.

"If they did fail, and we've had several over the years who have, we gave them swats with a board," he said. "Failing, even if it is just one week, was never tolerated at our school."

With his three best players out because of failing grades, Wood was down to just 17 players as he took his troops into the opening season game of 1941 against Spur.

Spur wasn't just another football team on the schedule. There was a rivalry there, at least from Wood's standpoint.

Woodrow Duckworth and Wood had competed for the head-coaching job at Spur in 1940. Wood had been assured the job only to lose it to Duckworth after a disgruntled board member raised a huge commotion about the fact that the board did not choose a coach from the Southwest Conference. The Spur School Board reversed its call and named Duckworth the head football coach.

Understandably upset, Wood took the head-coaching job at Rule when the 1940 school year ended. After his first season there, the new district assignments came out and Wood quickly went to Spur to set up a game.

Wood got his wish and, in September, Rule and Spur met in the 1941 season opener.

Before the game, Spur had a pep rally and Duckworth, being the good sport that he was, invited Wood and his team to join in the festivities. Wood agreed but, before he took his team to the pep rally, he dropped off four of his biggest players at a local motel.

"I brought in 13 of the smallest, scrawniest kids you could imagine and Spur had more than 40 big, fine-looking players," Wood said. "They made our team look like a small junior high team."

Duckworth told Wood's team not to worry, that he would try to make sure that none of Rule's players got hurt and that they would try to keep from running up the score on them.

As it turned out, it was Wood who would eventually have to call off the dogs. Rule ran up a score of 28-0 and, from there, never looked back.

Wood remembers that game as if it was last year's Super Bowl. To him, it was.

"I wanted to win that game so badly because I wanted to prove to people that I could coach," he said. "We could have beaten Notre Dame that day and it wouldn't have felt any better."

It was the classic case of David vs. Goliath and Wood's David prevailed.

"It's hard to explain what happened that day," he said. "They were a lot bigger than us and they outnumbered us almost 3-1. But we thought that we could beat them. And, anytime you think you can beat somebody, you've got a chance. People don't realize how much of sports - and life for that matter - is mental."

Grades played a key role in Wood's coaching philosophy. Winning football games is important, but getting a good education is even more important. Over the years, Wood has learned the value of education. As a coach, he tried to pass it on to his players.

"When I was growing up, nobody ever told me how important it was to get good grades," he said. "I probably could have gotten better grades if I would have tried harder, but there was no one who told me that I needed to."

In fact, it was Wood's father who urged him to quit school after the third grade.

"My dad was a great farmer," Wood said. "He thought that, after you learned to read and write, you didn't need any more education. He thought that if you went to the third grade, that was far enough."

Even during that time, Wood wasn't a regular in school.

"We were only allowed to go to school when it rained," he said. "When it rained, we couldn't pick cotton so my dad let us go to school."

School was relaxing compared to working the long hours in the cotton fields.

"We would work from the time the sun came up to the time the sun went down," he said. "When we would have a bad crop and have to go help the neighbors with their crops, we would only have to work 10 hours. Man, we thought that was a vacation."

Much of Wood's competitive drive comes from those days in the cotton fields, as even then he was concerned with "winning."

"I was always trying to outpick my brothers," he said. "I was always just trying to pick as much as I could every day and, when that day ended, I wanted to have more picked than anybody else. And I would, too. My brothers would stop in the afternoon to smoke and I didn't smoke so, while they smoked, I just kept on picking. I don't know why I did that. Looking back, I really don't know how much difference it would have made if my brothers had beaten me."

After those long hours in the fields, Wood knew that he was going to have to do something else with his life besides be a farmer.

"My dad thought that we were all going to be farmers," said Wood of himself and his seven other siblings. "But, to me, farming was too uncertain. There were years when we made good money at it but there were a lot of years when we'd get so much rain that it would ruin the crops and things would be awfully tight financially. I just didn't want to have to count on that for my living when it was so uncertain."

By the time Wood got to the seventh grade, his parents had leased a big, two-story house in town (Abilene) and then had sub-leased it out in order to make up for a bad crop the year before. It was during this year that Wood became interested in football.

"I'll never forget the first football game that I ever played," he said. "I was playing on the line and I just beat up the guy that was across from me. Just beat him to a pulp with my fists. There were no helmets at that time and the little leather headgear that was used didn't offer any type of protection. I feel bad about it now, but I didn't know anything about the game or how to play. I just went out there and did what I thought everybody else was doing and, to me, it looked like people were fighting."

Ironically enough, it was the only year that Wood ever played football.

"I wanted to play when I got to high school but my dad made me do all the milking when I would get home from practice," he said. "A full day of school, football practice and then all of the milking that I would do just got to be a little bit much for me so I quit playing football. Did you know that after I quit the team, my dad didn't make me milk the cows anymore?"

Although Wood gave the valedictory address when he graduated from Wylie in 1934, he says he still wasn't the top student in his class.

"I finished about in the middle of my class," Wood said. "But the boy who got valedictorian had gotten into a fight and I gave his speech for him."

The next year, Wood enrolled at Hardin-Simmons and brought his milk cow with him.

"I milked a cow for my room and board," he said. "I stayed with this family and they let me stay with them and eat with them for the milk that my cow gave."

Wood had gone to Hardin-Simmons on an athletic scholarship, playing football and basketball.

"I wasn't really that good of an athlete," he said. "I did okay, I guess. But there were a lot of athletes who were much better than I was. I was supposed to be on a football and basketball scholarship, but I didn't play much football."

While he couldn't quite play the game as well as he would have liked to, Wood was a master at getting the best out of his players, no matter what kind of hand he was dealt.

It was this type of challenge, this challenge of "trying to win with what you get" that kept Wood coaching high school football for 45 years.

"To be honest, I never did think about coaching in college or the NFL," he said. "At the college level, it's all recruiting. You recruit the right players and you're going to win. In the NFL, it's the same way with the draft. You draft the right players and you are going to be successful. In high school, however, you've got to win with what you have. You can't go out and recruit from other schools. What you have is what you've got and you've got to make the most of it. That's what I like about coaching high school football. It's just so unpredictable because the biggest and fastest teams don't always win. It's an area where coaching really can make a difference and I think that's why I stayed in it all those years."

After his retirement shortly after his 405th win in 1985, Wood has remained active in the Brownwood community. He keeps an office in downtown Brownwood and is a regular at the local coffee shop at 9:15 a.m. and 3:15 p.m. on weekdays.

"I don't know why I have an office," he said, smiling. "I don't ever do anything down there. But it gets me out of the house. I meet with some of my old friends for coffee every morning at 9:15 and again at 3:15 in the afternoon. It seems that there is always plenty to do. I'm the world's greatest waster of time. I can piddle a day away better than anyone you ever saw."

But, after winning 405 high school football games, maybe it is time to relax. So, Gordon, *How about them Duke Blue Devils?*

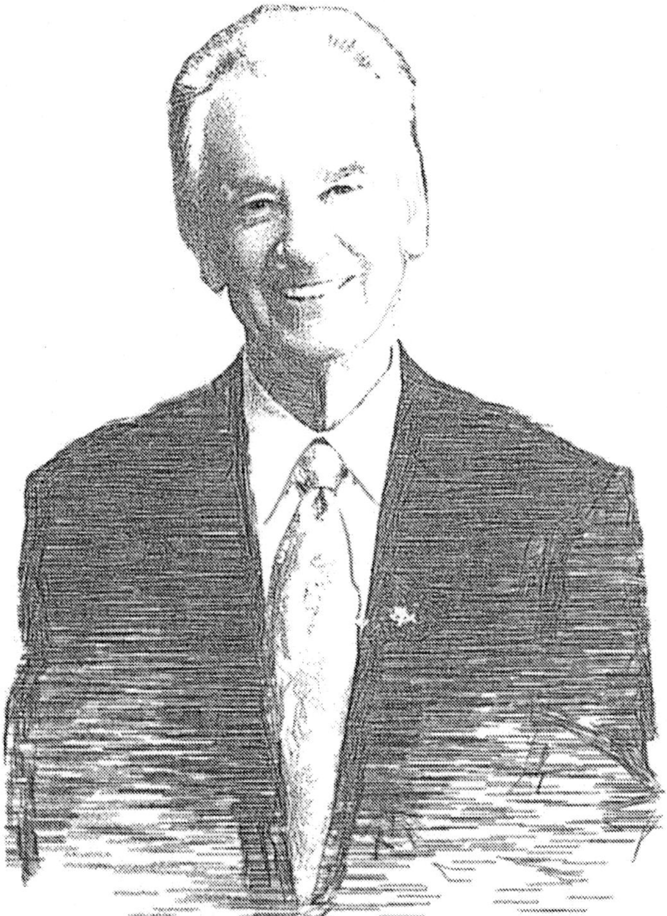

Zig Ziglar

Tips From The Top

Before we talked with Zig Ziglar, we wondered what he was like one-on-one. We had been to a few of his motivational seminars. We had heard his cassette tapes. But would he really be as enthusiastic over the phone as he was when he was giving a seminar? In other words, was the Z-man the real deal? The answers may surprise you.

The Wandering Generality. The Jack-of-All-Trades. We all know people like this. They drift from one project to another, one "Get-Rich-Quick Scheme" to another, one job to another and then wonder aloud why they aren't successful.

Oddly enough, Zig Ziglar was once a "Wandering Generality" himself before he found his niche as a motivational speaker. Today, Ziglar is known as one of the most positive people this side of the late Norman Vincent Peal. But it wasn't until he was in his late thirties that he received some advice that would change his life forever.

"The turning point of my career was when I got so broke that I had to go back to my roots and start selling cookware again," he said. "My dream was to be a motivational speaker but who was going to listen to a guy who was dead broke? I was having a hard time putting bread on my own table, much less trying to tell other people how to do it.

"I had been involved in 17 deals in five years. Seventeen! I had been involved in every 'Get-Rich-Quick Scheme' you could imagine and had come to the conclusion that there was no such thing.

"So I went back into the cookware business and my supervisor, a man I didn't particularly like, gave me some advice that literally changed my life. He said, 'Now, Zig, you're a great salesman but you are your own worst enemy. When somebody brags on you a little bit and tells you how good you are and then asks you to go to work for them, you immediately move on to another job or project or whatever. What you need to do is to re-establish yourself in this business. Why don't you do this: Tell yourself that, regardless of what comes down the pike, you are going to stay with this job for a year and that whatever other offers you get, you just tell them that you'll get back to them in a year's time. Meanwhile, you work just as hard as you can to re-establish yourself in this market over the next year and then you'll get more offers and better offers. But re-establish yourself first.'"

"That was in 1962 and it just made so much sense to me that I took his advice. After that first year, I was the number five salesman in American with our company. The next year, I was number one. I had re-established myself with better credentials and, from there, I could really start working toward my dream of becoming a speaker and started booking engagements whenever I could get them."

Ziglar, the 10th of 12 children, was born in the heart of the depression.

For some, this would be an obstacle. For Ziglar, it was a badge of honor.

"I had the advantage of growing up during the Great Depression," Ziglar recalls. "I was raised during some tough times. But, interestingly enough, I noticed that there were some people who were doing quite well, even in the depression. Driving nice cars, living in nice houses, wearing nice clothes, taking nice trips, the whole nine yards.

"The one thing that has remained consistent since that time is that, regardless of how good the economy is, some people seem to foul it up royally. And, no matter how bad it is, there are some people who will always seem to do well financially. So, the conclusion that I've come to is this: it's not really what is going on out there that counts but, rather, what is going on in your own mind that is really the determining factor. So, during those tough times, I never really made the mistake of blaming other things and other people and other events such as the economy, the government, the media and everything else. Sure, I fight with them, but I try to never blame them when things don't go well for me. I know what I have to do and that is to try to find out why things are going well for those people over there but not for me. I try to emulate the successful."

Ten years later, in 1972, something else would happen that would change Ziglar's life forever. On July 4, 1972, he accepted Christ as his personal Savior. It was on that day when he realized that all the motivational books in the world weren't going to be good enough to get him to heaven.

"When I accepted Christ into my life on July 4, 1972, all of the years of learning and studying came into focus," he said. "By that time, my career was going pretty well, but

I was still broke and in debt. I had made some pretty bad financial moves at that point and when I started realizing what God had to say, along with the other knowledge I had gained, then everything began to fall into place. I realized that I had confused knowledge with wisdom. It was on that day that I learned the difference between the two and realized that knowledge wasn't really the key to success. If it was, everybody with a Ph.D. would be rich and successful and every high school dropout would be poor and miserable. I knew that this wasn't the case.

"Knowledge comes from books. Wisdom comes from the Bible. True success comes when a person is able to combine the two and, on July 4, 1972, that's what I began to do."

Ziglar, now in his late 60s, still has the energy and enthusiasm of a man a third of his age. He is normally up early, reading scripture and getting two hours of reading in before his wife wakes up.

"Some days I read three hours and then some days I read a little bit more than that," he said. "But I try to read whenever I can. When I'm sitting at an airport, I'm either reading or writing. I get up in the morning about an hour or two before my wife does. Then I'll go downstairs and put a couple of pieces of toast in the toaster and have a cup of coffee and I'll read the Bible for about 40 to 45 minutes. Then, I'll get the newspaper and start reading that. When I'm in the middle of a book project I'll get up and write for a few hours before my wife gets up and that gives us a little bit more time together later in the day."

Ziglar is not one for small talk. His schedule won't allow it. In fact, he said, learning to say "No" is a large part of being successful.

"Obviously, I get a lot of interruptions," he said. "The only ones I really respond to are those who have a real need. I am not much for talking to people who just want to talk. My administrative assistant screens a lot of calls and just because someone calls doesn't necessarily mean that I'm going to talk to them. The time is simply not there."

Then there are the countless requests for book endorsements.

"The other thing that I have to do is to tell people 'No' who want me to endorse their books. In the past six days alone, I have had no less than 10 books that people have wanted me to endorse. I can't endorse every book that people want me to endorse simply because, to endorse a book, I have to read it. And I can't read 10 books in six days. So, I have to tell some people 'No.' I've got to be careful because, if I endorse a book that turns out to be against the things that I believe, then I have lost a part of me.

"I try to take most requests in stride and give a reason when I can't do something. Some people don't understand but, at that point, it becomes their problem."

Another key to success, Ziglar added, is knowing the true meaning of the word "successful."

"Basically, there are certain things that everybody wants to have," he said. "They want to be happy, healthy and reasonably prosperous. They want to have friends, peace of mind, good family relationships and they want to have hope. Most people want to have some of the things that money can buy and all of the things that money can't buy. Money will buy nice clothes, a nice house, a nice car, nice golf equipment and a membership to the country club. I like all those things but I love the things that money can't buy.

"It'll buy you a companion, but it won't buy you a friend. It'll buy me a house, but it won't buy me a home. It'll buy me a good time, but it won't buy me peace of mind. It will buy me a bed but it won't buy me a good night's sleep. When you start looking at it that way, it's pretty easy to determine which one is greed or blind ambition versus which one is a legitimate direction to go in.

"If I make millions of dollars but destroy my health, what have I got? If I go to the top of my profession, but destroy my relationship with my beautiful wife, then what have I got? These are questions that everybody has to ask themselves."

To watch one of Ziglar's presentations is to see a man with enormous energy. Off stage, Ziglar is much the same way.

"Sure, I do get tired sometimes," Ziglar said. "But I don't think that I ever really get depressed. I do get a little discouraged at times but, in 99 times out of 100, that happens when I'm extremely tired. Now, when I get tired, that manifests itself in a loss of patience and my energy level is a little lower than normal and I think, 'Well, I guess I just can't do as much as I thought I could.' But I honestly believe that my worst days are a lot of people's best days.

"When I'm really, really tired, I will take a nap or when I have a book tour and I have been going hot and heavy all day and have a 30-minute drive to a second interview, I'll sleep about 20 minutes along the way and I'll feel energized when I get to that second interview. I also take walks and that seems to revive me. One thing that I've learned over the years is that I never want to make a decision when I'm tired because my decisions won't be as good at that point."

One decision that Ziglar probably didn't make when he was tired was his decision to, in his friend's words, "re-establish himself."

Following that sound advice proved to make him more than a Wandering Generality. It helped to make him one of the greatest motivational speakers in world.

The Man in the Arena

"It is not the critic who counts, not the man who points out how the strong man stumbled, or where the doer of deeds could have done better. The credit belongs to the man who is actually in the arena; whose face is marred by the dust and sweat and blood; who strives valiantly; who errs and comes short again and again; who knows the great enthusiasms, the great devotions and spends himself in a worthy cause; who at the best, knows in the end the triumph of high achievement, and who, at worst, if he fails, at least fails while daring greatly; so that his place shall never be with those cold and timid souls who know neither victory or defeat."

-THEODORE ROOSEVELT
(Paris Sorbonne, 1910)

Printed in the United States
26011LVS00002B/1-63